GO *by the* BOOK

GO
by the
BOOK

THOUGHTS ON BIBLICAL THEMES

Robert Davidson

Series Editor: Duncan B Forrester

SAINT ANDREW PRESS
EDINBURGH

First published in 1996 by
SAINT ANDREW PRESS
121 George Street, Edinburgh EH2 4YN

ISBN 0 7152 0710 5

British Library Cataloguing in Publication Data
A catalogue record for this book
is available from the British Library.

ISBN 0715207105

Quotations in this book are taken in general from *The Revised English Bible*, © Oxford University Press and Cambridge University Press 1989. *The Revised English Bible* is a revision of *The New English Bible*; *The New English Bible* New Testament was first published by the Oxford and Cambridge University Presses in 1961, and the complete Bible in 1970.

Cover design by Mark Blackadder.
Cover photograph by Walter Bell.
Printed by BPC-AUP Aberdeen Ltd.

Contents

Series Editor's Introduction

ALL down the ages Christians have reflected on their faith and its bearing on life. These reflections have taken a great variety of forms, but one of the most common has been the sermon. For generations notable preachers were well-known public figures, and books of sermons were a well-known literary genre. In many places people queued to hear great preachers, whose sermons were reported in the press, and discussed and dissected afterwards. Sermons launched great movements of mission, and revival, and social change. Sometimes influential preachers were imprisoned by the authorities so that their disturbing challenge should not be heard.

Nowhere was this tradition more lively than in Scotland. But today, some people say, the glory has departed. If you want to find great preaching today, the critics say, go to Africa, or Latin America, or to Black churches in the States. No longer in Scotland do people pack in their hundreds into huge churches to hear great preachers. The sermon seems to have lost its centrality in Scottish life. The conviction and the emotional surcharge that once sustained a great succession of notable preachers seems hard to find today. Has secularisation destroyed the appetite for sermons? Has the modern questioning of authority eroded the preaching office? Do Christians no longer reflect on their faith, or do they do it in other and newer ways?

This series of books shows that the tradition of preaching is still very much alive and well. It has changed, it is true, and it has adapted to new circumstances and new challenges. It is not the same as it was in the long afterglow of the Victorian pulpit. Reflection by the Scots on their faith, as these books illustrate, is perhaps more varied than it was in the past, and their sermons are briefer. But Scottish preaching is still passionate, thoughtful, biblical, challenging, and deeply concerned with the relevance of the gospel to the needs of today's world.

The reflections on the Christian faith in these books are challenging, disturbing, nourishing. They proclaim a Word that is alive and active, and penetrates to the depths of things, a Word that speaks of hope and worth, of forgiveness and new beginnings, of justice, peace and love. And so they invite the reader to engage afresh with the everlasting gospel.

Duncan B Forrester
EDINBURGH

In Memoriam
Revd Arthur H Gray DD
through whose preaching
a profound biblical simplicity
touched many lives

Introduction

IN his poem 'The Incarnate One', Edwin Muir talks about

> ... *the Word made flesh here is made word again,*
> *A word made word in flourish and in arrogant crook.*

'The Word made flesh' too often loses its directness and freshness when it is tamed or distorted in the flourish of the spoken, preached word. It is in danger of suffering a worse fate when the passion of the spoken, preached word is turned into cold print. But with the loss of directness, as the spoken word becomes the written word, there may also be gain. At least some of the personal and distracting habits which haunt the pulpit disappear!

The sermons in this small volume have been preached over many years and in many different settings – in town and country churches, in university chapels, on radio and television. They suffer because they are not earthed in the day-to-day relationship between a minister and the people to whom he ministers. That is the penalty of a lifetime spent in academic cloisters instead of in the parish ministry. They represent where I have been in my spiritual pilgrimage and where I am after years of trying to come to terms with the Bible, and in particular with that part of it which Christians call the Old Testament. I am not sure that I *have* come to terms with it. I suspect that I may never do so. To 'Go by the Book' does not mean accepting the Bible as a handy text book containing one neat easily spelled out picture of God which can be found in every passage in the book. Often we have to listen to voices arguing with one another, as well as with God. Against this background the sermons – all of which have as their starting point a text or passage from the Old Testament – reflect in different ways what have come to be for me two major concerns:

1 They express a conviction concerning the eternal mystery which is at the heart of life, a mystery which in the end is only deepened when for Christians the veil is cast aside and we look into the face of Jesus. All true faith will cherish this mystery, not seek to destroy it. We do well to listen to Edwin Muir's words of warning when God becomes

> ... *three angry letters in a book*
> *And there the logical hook*
> *On which the mystery is impaled and bent*
> *Into an ideological instrument.*

Too often we want and seek to use religion, instead of humbling ourselves before its mystery.

2 They express the assurance that this mystery accompanies us through life, even when we are least aware of that presence. There is a hand laid on our shoulder. This does not guarantee a comfortable journey with all the sharp edges of life smoothed away. Very often it increases our questions. It may mean living with some questions unanswered and others unanswerable. It means accepting within the orbit of faith that there is a place for honest doubt. But if I mistake not, the mystery, the presence and the questioning are part of the rich tapestry of faith to which the Bible bears witness.

Robert Davidson

Go by the Book

NOT so long ago we celebrated here in Scotland 'The Year of the Bible'. The celebrations took many forms. There was a large scale publicity campaign. On buses and on hoardings, in shop windows and in churches, posters appeared with the short, snappy slogan: 'Go by the Book'. It was an invitation to which many people responded, if increased sales of the Bible were anything to go by. Yet I wonder how many people who accepted that invitation found that to try to 'go by the book' raised as many questions as it answered. Instead of offering us one simple, easily understood message, the Bible asks us to listen to many different voices, sometimes apparently saying contradictory things.

Our Old Testament lesson was part of a famous passage from the book of Ecclesiastes. They are the words of a man who had taken a long, cool look at life and discovered it to be a rich tapestry of contrasting experiences. There is, he says:

> *a time to be born and a time to die;*
> *a time to plant and a time to uproot;*
> *a time to kill and a time to heal;*
> *a time to break down and a time to build up;*
> *a time to weep and a time to laugh;*
> *a time for mourning and a time for dancing;*
> *… … …*
> *a time for silence and a time for speech;*

a time to love and a time to hate;
a time for war and a time for peace.

~ Ecclesiastes 3:2-4, 7-8 ~

As the varied colours in this tapestry are woven together, quite clearly they make fascinating God-given sense – or do they? They don't; not to the author of this book. Fascinating in its variety, enjoyable – yes, that is life, says Ecclesiastes; but if you ask what it all means, you end up with a large question mark. Presumably God knows what it all means, but he hasn't chosen to tell us.

This is the God who '*has made everything to suit its time; moreover he has given* [us] *a sense of past and future, but no comprehension of God's work from beginning to end*' (3:11). How strangely at variance this is with other voices in the Bible who seem to know, and to speak and to live with untroubled certainty. A prophet may stand before the people and declare, 'Thus says the LORD'; this man shrugs his shoulders and says, 'Who knows?'

Or take another issue. We find Ecclesiastes looking at a society in which the poor are being denied their rights, where bribery is rife and where justice for many is only a pipe dream. There is no point, he says, in getting upset about it; it's the system and you can't beat the system, particularly the bureaucracy which is a past master at passing the buck (5:8). Turn to the Old Testament prophets, however, and they do get upset, upset in the name of God, and demand that the poor be treated with compassion and given their rights; and if that means turning the system upside down, so be it.

Again, you won't go far in your reading of the Old Testament before you hear voices telling you, 'Obey the LORD and you will reap rich, tangible rewards in this life'. This is God's world – in it the righteous flourish and the wicked come to a sticky end. Honour the LORD, and you will gain the ancient Hebrew equivalent of a healthy bank balance, and you will always be able to wine and dine in the best places in town. But Ecclesiastes is only one of several voices who say to us, 'That is not true'. The same fate comes to the righteous and to the wicked, to good and bad alike, to those who are devotedly religious and to those who are not. You can honour the LORD and die in poverty; you can ignore God and be a paid up member of the millionaires' club.

You must not think, however, that Ecclesiastes is a solitary dissident challenging the otherwise accepted party line, the one cuckoo in an otherwise comfortable theological nest. He is no more than a clear, warning sign of something we shall find facing us right across the Bible if only we are prepared to discard our pious blinkers and read it honestly and intelligently. Turn to the Psalms, for example, and you will find yourself listening to the words of people who look back across the history of their nation, who ponder their own experience, and see from beginning to end the inescapable goodness and steadfast love of God; people whose natural response to life is to shout 'Hallelujah' – praise the LORD (*eg* Psalms 100, 136). But there are other voices, the voices of those who in perplexity and bitterness can only say, 'How long, O LORD .... Why have you forsaken us …?', whose natural response to life is to turn to God and scream, 'Wake up!' (*eg* Psalms 13, 74). We hear the voices of those, like many people today, who have been brought up in a strong tradition of faith, yet find that it no longer makes sense of their own experience. As a Psalmist complains:

We have heard for ourselves, God,
our forefathers have told us
what deeds you did in their time,
all your hand accomplished in days of old.
…   …   …
Yet you have rejected and humbled us
and no longer lead our armies to battle.

3

You have forced us to retreat before the foe,
and our enemies have plundered us at will.
You have given us up to be slaughtered like sheep
and scattered us among the nations.
You sold your people for next to nothing
and had no profit from the sale.

~ Psalms 44:1-2, 9-12 ~

By this time you may well be thinking – that, of course, is only what we might expect from the Old Testament. It is an untidy, sprawling book, telling us of people who either couldn't make up their minds what they believed, or did not know how to express their beliefs coherently. That is why we have been given the New Testament – to tidy up the mess! Is it? Have you ever read the New Testament as a whole, and its witness, or rather witnesses, to Jesus? Have you ever seriously wondered how the picture of Jesus which you find in the Gospel of John fits in with the picture of Jesus which is there in Mark's Gospel? In John's Gospel, Jesus from the very beginning is hailed by the disciples as the long-expected Jewish Messiah, but in Mark's Gospel … ?

Or take the letters which Paul wrote to the early Christian communities. They are in many respects models of pastoral concern; they bear consistent witness to the central certainties of the Christian faith. Paul, however, was far from being consistent. On certain things – for example the possible return of Jesus during his lifetime – Paul was prepared to change his mind. If you can read the New Testament without being struck by its richly varied witnesses to Jesus, if you can read it without being aware of the many loose ends lying around within it, then I suggest that you go and read it again.

The greatest disservice we can do to the Bible is to call it 'The Word of God' and assume that this means that we shall find within it everywhere exactly the same teaching, the same beliefs. Herein lies the basic error of many brands of fundamentalism – and other religious-isms – not that they hold to certain theories about the infallibility of the Bible, whatever that means, but that they pluck certain statements from the Bible, weave them together into some kind of orthodoxy, and then proceed to read the Bible as if that creed were there to be discovered in every verse from beginning to end. You cannot do this without destroying the Bible.

There is within the Bible a rich variety of voices and we shall never understand it unless we are prepared to listen to these many voices, speaking to us out of different circumstances and experiences: voices of serenity and of hurt, voices of quiet acceptance and vigorous protest, voices of certainty and bewilderment, voices often arguing with one another, and sometimes with God. This is not something to regret, or something which is destructive of faith.

Let me suggest two reasons why we should rejoice in this and welcome it as helpful to faith:

1　The many voices within the Bible have enabled this library of books to speak meaningfully across the centuries to people facing the bewildering variety of life's experiences; and in particular to people trying to respond to the challenge of discipleship in different centuries, in different countries and in changing circumstances. I once had the privilege of officiating at the marriage service of a near relative. Within a few weeks of the wedding his wife walked out to move in with another man with whom she had been involved even before the wedding. A few months later we received a Christmas card from that relative, a card on which he had lavished his not inconsiderable artistic skill. On the front, in his own distinctive script, there was written that passage from Ecclesiastes, including the lines:

a time to weep and a time to laugh;
a time for mourning and a time for dancing;
... ...
a time to embrace and a time to abstain from embracing;
... ...
a time for silence and a time for speech;
a time to love and a time to hate ....

A few weeks later I met him, thanked him for his Christmas card and asked him why he had chosen to put on it that passage from Ecclesiastes.

He replied, 'It is the only part of the Bible which continues to make sense to me at this moment'.

At that moment he was finding it very difficult to come to terms with some of the powerful affirmations about God in the Bible. As he struggled to pick up the pieces of a broken life, much of what was in the Bible rang no bells for him. But that passage did; it was where he was. When a few years later he happily remarried, that same passage was, at his request, central to the wedding service.

Let me give you another example. I once had to read and examine a PhD thesis on the subject of the 'poor' in the Psalms. Though I did not know this when I first read it, it was the work of a Brazilian pastor whose ministry had been amidst the crippling poverty and economic destitution of the shanty towns around San Paulo. He had been deeply influenced by the thinking of Latin American liberation theologians. He was arguing the case that the 'poor' in the Psalms were nearly always the economically deprived and the politically powerless people in ancient Israel. By a selective use of material from the Psalms and elsewhere in the Bible, he argued for the legitimacy of violence as a Christian response to otherwise unchangeable oppressive political and social regimes. I was not wholly convinced by his arguments. I was not convinced that he had fully explored the wide range of meanings associated with the words translated 'the poor' in the Psalms: yet who was I, living in comparative freedom, security and affluence, to deny that there might be insights into the biblical message given to him in his ministry, insights to which I had been blind. The Bible had been speaking to him and to his people in their situation, words of challenge and hope.

Because the Bible contains within it the words of people wrestling with different challenges and experiences, seeking to respond to a vision of God's revelation as it plays upon the particular circumstance of their life, that is what makes it possible for each of us to hear words which speak to our own situation, as we seek to open our lives to that same vision.

2 It is this rich variety within the Bible which ensures that the Christian faith offers us a God worthy to be worshipped and served. We all have our own favourite ways of talking about God, but let us never forget that none of the words we use can ever be adequate to describe the greatness and the mystery of God.

I once came out of a large religious gathering feeling thoroughly depressed, unable to share in the evident enthusiasm of most of the other people who had been there. They had been enthralled by the preacher. His words had been lucid and powerful, packed with emotional dynamite. He had left no one in any doubt as to who God was, what he offered to each one of us and what he expected from us in return. But for me there was something missing. The preacher could have been an extremely well-informed and skillful salesman, talking me into buying a new car, kitchen units or double-glazing. The presentation could hardly be faulted. I knew exactly what was on offer; and that was what worried me. Something was missing. Call it what you like – a sense of mystery, a feeling for the majesty, the otherness, the transcendence of God – that had disappeared; there was no room for it in the glossy packaging. I thought of some of the hesitant, stumbling words in the Bible on the lips of people who claimed to have met God and who emerged from that experience shaken and shattered, hardly knowing what to say. I thought of others who had an overwhelming sense of being grasped by the love of God, and knew that this was only the beginning of a story which could never be fully expressed in mere human words.

Nowhere is this better expressed than in the Letter to the Ephesians. Here is someone who claims to have been given an 'insight into the mystery of Christ' (3:4, Revised Standard Version). But this does not mean that he is claiming to have solved a religious puzzle, or that he has the last word to say about God. He talks about barriers which have been swept away, about how both Jews and non Jews can now equally share in God's new family. The barriers have been swept away, not because they have sat down and hammered out together a common creed, but because they have received 'the good news of the *unfathomable* riches of Christ' (3:8). They share together in the love of God which has come to them in Christ; and when he thinks of that love, Paul – or whoever wrote this letter – is on his knees praying that all may share it and 'be strong to grasp what is the breadth and length and height and depth of Christ's love, and to know it, *though it is beyond knowledge*' (3:18-19). It is this 'beyond' that we ignore at our peril.

It is usually the people who are 'furthest ben' with God who know how far they still have to go. If you wish a God of no surprises, a God whom you can coldly and fully describe, then

I suggest that you better look elsewhere than in the Bible. I wouldn't go by this book! For this book offers you another God, a God who, in the words of a Jewish writer who survived the horrors of Auschwitz, ' … is in man, even in suffering, even in misfortune, even in evil. God is everywhere … God does not wait for man at the end of the road … he accompanies him there. More than that, He *is* the road ….'

But you don't describe this God in any one neat set of words. You are invited to travel with him, believing that he travels with you. To 'go by the book' is to be willing to set out on that journey.

❖

Changing Symbols

*... the L*ORD *was not in the wind ... the L*ORD *was not in the earthquake ... the L*ORD *was not in the fire.*

~ 1 Kings 19:11-12 ~

BUT he ought to have been! Everything that the prophet Elijah had been brought up to believe insisted that God ought to have been in the wind ... in earthquake ... and in fire. For centuries it had been known in Israel that God was present in such things – in the wind which had swept aside the waters of the Red Sea to turn it into a pathway to freedom for an enslaved people; on that mountain, shuddering in the violence of a thunder and lightning storm, the mountain which quaked when God met with these same people to give direction to their lives; in that bush which was on fire when Moses came face to face with his call to service; in that pillar of fire by night which guided the people through the darkness of the wilderness.

Wind ... earthquake ... fire, traditional symbols, hallowed symbols of God's presence in the midst of his people. Who indeed better than Elijah to know in his own personal experience that God was in fire. Alone on Mount Carmel Elijah had thrown down the gauntlet to the devotees of a rival religion. He had staked all on a decisive vindication of the power of his God in a test of dramatic simplicity. Altar and sacrifice prepared; but who would light the fire to consume the offering? The prophets of that rival religion used all the tricks of their trade in a vain attempt to call down fire from heaven. Elijah then prays:

'LORD God of Abraham, of Isaac, and of Israel, let it be known today that you are God in Israel and that I am your servant and have done all these things at your command. Answer me, LORD, answer me and let this people know that you, LORD, are God and that it is you who have brought them back to their allegiance.' The fire of the LORD fell, consuming the whole-offering, the wood, the stones, and the earth, and licking up the water in the trench.

~ 1 Kings 18:36-38 ~

This was Elijah's moment of triumph; but after triumph the bitter truth. Queen Jezebel, a remarkable woman, singularly unimpressed by any reported display of divine pyrotechnics at Mount Carmel and livid at the liquidation by Elijah of her co-religionists, leaves Elijah in no doubt that the nation was not big enough to contain both him and her. His life threatened, Elijah flees south into the desert, back to the traditional mountain meeting place of God and his people. What he expected to find there we shall never know; what he did find was surprising and disturbing. At this traditional home of Israel's faith, he found that the familiar symbols of that faith, symbols shaped and hallowed by tradition and experience, were no longer adequate to convey to him the reality of God's presence:

… the LORD was not in the wind … not in the earthquake … not in the fire.

But he was there; there in 'the still small voice', which may be more accurately translated as 'the sound of a faint whisper' or 'the sound of a fine silence', the kind of silence so absolute that you can, as it were, hear it. Elijah is not being taught that God is to be found in the realm of the spirit rather than in the world of nature; nor is he discovering that God is 'within' rather than 'without', in his inner conscience rather than in the world out there. Silence is just as much natural and out there as wind, earthquake and fire. No, Elijah is facing a much more disturbing and challenging contrast. On the one hand there is silence, on the other the noise and turbulence of wind, earthquake and fire. These traditional symbols had taken Elijah so far in his spiritual pilgrimage, now he was faced with so enlarging his vision and his experience, that he would be open to a God coming to him in a totally different and contrasting symbol.

Elijah's experience is not uncommon. It finds its echo in the lives of many people today, people not only outside but also within the church and the Christian family. There are people for whom traditional ways of worship and Christian living no longer ring bells; people for whom much of our traditional talk about God and prayer is becoming ever more remote; people for whom many of the great words and affirmations of the Bible are like meaningless echoes from the past; people for whom many hitherto accepted patterns of Christian conduct, of right and wrong, are increasingly up for questioning. There are perplexed people who look for God and find him singularly absent where people of faith in the past have declared him to be powerfully present. Perhaps we all share something of this experience. It is an uncomfortable experience. It has led many to the point where Christian faith has crumbled or has been dismissed as no longer relevant.

We may respond to this experience in different ways. We may struggle to avoid facing what is happening, desperately hanging on to the familiar because in the familiar we feel safe. As for the nagging questions and doubts, forget them. When the familiar is threatened we are tempted to think only in terms of loss – loss of faith, loss of certainty and loss of purpose in life. Indeed there are those who in sincerity will try to convince you that this is the only true response, that anything else is the work of the devil. We must continue to believe in God in the traditional words and ways; we must continue to serve God in the well-tried patterns – and we can, if only we try hard enough. We are invited to be like the Queen in *Alice in Wonderland*, faced with a disbelieving Alice:

'I can't believe *that*,' said Alice.

'Can't you?' the Queen said, in a pitying tone. 'Try again, draw a deep breath and shut your eyes.'

Alice laughed, 'There's no use trying,' she said. 'One can't believe impossible things.'

'I dare say you haven't had much practice,' said the Queen. 'When I was your age, I always did it for half an hour. Why sometimes I've believed as many as six impossible things before breakfast.'

There are many people today who have tried. They have drawn a deep breath, they have shut their eyes and still in honesty say 'I can't believe that'. Among them are some of the most thoughtful, sensitive and caring people. If we have tried and still find ourselves saying about parts of the Christian tradition 'I can't believe that', where do we go? Is this loss of faith? Perhaps ... but ought we not rather think of it in terms of liberation, of being set free from the tyranny of symbols which are no longer able to carry life's meaning for us, set free to meet God anew? God does not die when some of our traditional ways of talking about him and worshipping him die. Some of the symbols within which we have encased God may have to die, if we are to have a continuingly meaningful faith.

... the LORD was not in the wind ... not in the earthquake ... not in the fire

But he was there! On a small mound, not many miles from where Elijah fought his battle against the devotees of a rival faith, there stood just over a hundred years ago one of the greatest biblical scholars of his day. He was there in Palestine, mapping the terrain, attempting, among other things, to fix clearly the sites of many of the ancient cities mentioned in the Bible. In his diary for the day there is this entry: 'This mound would make an excellent site for a city, but there are no traces here of any ancient settlement.' In fact he was literally standing on the top of several cities and on the surface of the ground around him there were tell-tale signs which would have sent any modern archaeologist post haste to the most likely Foundation with a plea for money to mount a large scale dig. Through no fault of his own he was looking for the wrong things, for the traces of ruined buildings, the remains of walls, for *objets d'art*. He was blind to the significance of the tiny fragments of broken pottery on the ground at his feet. What he knew, what he had been trained to look for, what he expected to see, prevented him from seeing what was really there.

In many fields of knowledge, advance only comes through questioning and doubting what has until then been taken for granted. The creative scholar or research worker is the person who leaps beyond what he or she has been taught, beyond what others see, to find a new, a more meaningful and a more convincing interpretation of what has been there all the time. It is no different with faith. Sometimes the real enemy of faith is not our doubts, but our certainties, these terrifying certainties which claim to know, if not all about God, at least exactly how he works, precisely how and in what ways he touches our life and the lives of other people. It is, of course, comforting to have God neatly controlled and channelled into the type of Christian fellowship or experience which suits our temperament, into *our* church, into words that warm our hearts, whether they be the words of the Authorised Version of the Bible or the Songs of Zion or words with a more modern ring such as 'the man for others' or 'the secular city'. But the channels we have dug may have to burst before we can know the full sweep of the majesty and the mystery of God. The trouble is not that what we know is necessarily untrue, but in our yielding to the temptation to exalt the little we do know into the whole truth. If we are not prepared to question what we know, not prepared to be surprised by God, then we have still a lot to learn, and to unlearn, about the meaning of faith.

... the LORD was not in the wind ... not in the earthquake ... not in the fire.

Elijah would hardly have been surprised if he had been. But the Lord was there, surprisingly there in the silence.

It is only the dullness of familiarity which prevents us from seeing that the greatest surprise, the largest question mark placed against people's religious symbols and longings, was, and is, Jesus. He didn't – and he doesn't – fit. To many of the most deeply religious of his contemporaries, he was to the very end a bitter disappointment. This could hardly be the truth about the God they had known, the God they sought.

They were looking for a God-sent king, a descendant of the once great Davidic royal family; they were given a baby born in the most obscure circumstances into a village carpenter's family – surely not!

They believed in a God of righteousness; they met a man who shunned the respectable company of the guardians of morality and hobnobbed with people of doubtful repute – surely not!

They worshipped a God who made his home in the midst of his people in the temple in Jerusalem; they faced a man who created a public uproar in the courtyards of that temple – surely not!

They were awaiting a God who would lead his people to triumph over their pagan oppressors and enemies; they saw instead a man dying on a public gibbet at the hands of these enemies – surely not!

If one thing was crystal clear, it was that the God they sought was not in this man. Yet this is what the New Testament writers, one and all, challenge us to believe. They have no one way of saying this to us. They use many different pictures, many different words. Always, if we would hear them right, we must realise that they are straining at the very boundary of human language to try to communicate something which can never be coldly encapsulated into any set of human words. We shall never understand what they are saying to us, unless we realise that they are telling us of a surprise, the wonder of which never left them.

We left Elijah facing God in the silence. But he had something else to learn. When, fleeing from an irate Queen, he came to the traditional home of Israel's faith, he came in near despair. He had played his ace against paganism, only to have it trumped by a Queen. He came disappointed, filled with self pity. He took great pains to point out to God that he had done everything he could, against formidable odds. He had given his all. He was appealing for sympathy, for a word of approval. He didn't get it. Into the silence there came a sharp accusing voice, as if speaking to a deserter. 'What are you doing here, Elijah?' Go back, go back and fight again for what you believe. Go back, taking with you the broken fragments of some of the things you once believed, go back doubt-less with many questions still unanswered, but go back.

So it is with Jesus, the man who was such an unwelcome sur-prise even to many of those who knew him best. He walked along the shore of a lake, looked some fishermen in the eye and said, 'Come, follow me … ' – and they went. Although they had many shocks in store, and many of their ideas had to be turned upside down, they continued to follow. They found they had no option. It is this same surprising Jesus who confronts us along the differing roads of our lives. Sometimes, I believe, we fail to find him because we are looking for the wrong things; sometimes we fail to see him because our picture of him is already too firmly fixed in our minds. We map out where we expect him to be, and he has a disconcerting habit of disappearing off our maps. But he is there; often in strange guise, meeting us in unfamiliar ways, surprising us, challenging us to come out from behind many of our comfortable assumptions, saying anew, 'Come, follow me ...', and keep following even when the way ahead seems uncertain, even when we don't have all the answers, perhaps particularly when we can't claim to have all the answers. For Elijah 'the LORD was not in the wind ... not in the earthquake ... not in the fire'. *But he was there,* challengingly there, in the silence.

The Mystery
which meets us

'How awesome is this place! This is none other than the house of God; it is the gateway to heaven.'

~ Genesis 28:17 ~

HAVE your ever heard someone say something and thought to yourself, 'Well, well, I never expected to hear him, or her, say anything like that. It's so out of character'. That is very much how I react when I listen to these words of Jacob as he woke up in a night disturbed by a strange dream at Bethel. He didn't know what to make of it! All he could say was: 'How awesome is this place. This is none other than the house of God; it is the gateway to heaven.' Nothing in Jacob's life up to that point prepares us for such words. Jacob was a young man on the make. He knew what he wanted in life and he was determined to get it. Anyone who stood in his way was liable to be brushed aside. He would have known his way around, and prospered, in our 'enterprise' society. There was a tired, hungry brother conned one day into giving up his rights as the oldest son in the family: and if you argue that that brother Esau ought to have known better than to give up his rights for a bowl of soup, there is seldom any excuse for exploiting another person's weaknesses for your own selfish ends.

There was that day when, with a sympathetic push from a doting mother, he had no scruples about deceiving his old blind father. Jacob was on the make, rather a nasty character. He was doing quite well for himself, till relationships in the family became so tense that it was thought advisable that he should take a long holiday in another country. If he could pick up a good, sensible wife while he was there, so much the better.

So Jacob packed his bags, said his farewells and set off. He hadn't gone far, not much more than fifty miles, when he came to a place he was to call Bethel, 'house of God'. There something unexpected happened. A new dimension entered his life. He found himself face to face with an experience which he did not know how to handle. This was something for which he had not bargained. He did not immediately know how he could turn it to his own advantage. There was only one word to describe it – 'awesome'. It took him out of himself. It questioned whether life did centre only on himself, his own ambitions, his own desires. He was there in a place where everything seemed to be speaking to him of God, of a mystery beyond his understanding: *'This is none other than the house of God; it is the gateway to heaven.'* Shouldn't this be our experience as we gather for worship in church, in a place where there is so much pointing us to the mystery which surrounds our lives?

There is a baptismal font, reminding us that we are here, members of the church, not because we have any right to be here, not because we want God, but because God, in the mystery of his love, wants us: reminding us, not least if we truly believe in infant baptism, that before we can give anything to God, he gives himself graciously and freely to us.

There is a table round which we gather from time to time as members of God's family, not because we deserve to come to that family table, but because we accept an invitation to share together what God offers us in and through Jesus.

There is a lectern and on it a book; not any book, not at times the easiest of books to read or to understand, but the book through which people in all walks of life have found God speaking to them, and have learned that wherever they are in their lives and whatever they face, they are not on their own.

There are stained glass windows. They are not there merely for decoration or to add colour to the scene or to commemorate their donor. Through the vision and imagination of artists and the skill of craftsmen, they tell us in form and in colour the same story which is there in font, in table and in book, the story on which we are invited to base our life.

We rightly pay homage in our Reformed and Presbyterian tradition to the sermon, to the spoken word, but words can at times be coldly inadequate. All around us, as we gather for worship, there are these visible, silent witnesses which can touch our senses with the experience of wonder and awe, reminding us that 'this is none other than the house of God; it is the gateway to heaven'.

What happened to Jacob that night, however, did not suddenly make him into a new and totally different person. The leopard does not change its spots all that easily. He had been accustomed to driving a hard bargain, accustomed to using other people for his own ends.

It is hardly surprising, therefore, that once he had time to gather his thoughts, Jacob began to wonder how he could use this mysterious God for his own ends:

'If God will be with me, if he will protect me on my journey and give me food to eat and clothes to wear, so that I come back safely to my father's house, then the LORD shall be my God.'

~ Genesis 28:20-21 ~

Perhaps he felt he was on to a good thing. If this mysterious God kept his side of the bargain, then life would work out as Jacob hoped it would and it would be only reasonable for him to give God something in return. Face to face with the mystery and wonder of God, Jacob had still a lot to learn, and to unlearn, before the true meaning of what had happened that night could shape and control his life. He did not find it easy. There were struggles ahead, but he had caught a glimpse of what lies at the heart of worship.

Someone used to come to see me occasionally. Whenever he entered the room I used to say to myself, 'Here we go again'. I knew exactly what was going to happen. For the next fifteen or twenty minutes I would not need to say any more than 'yes' or 'no' or perhaps an occasional 'really!' There would be no opportunity to say any more! I was going to hear all about what he had been doing and all about what he hoped to do. There would be up-to-date news about his family, their travels, their successes and their problems. It would all come pouring out. The torrent of words would then suddenly cease. He would say, 'Thank you for listening; I must be going'. And he went!

I have no doubt it did him good to come and talk. He wasn't, however, in the least interested in me; I was just a useful sounding board. I wonder whether there are not times when we are in danger of treating God like that. We come to him with our prayers – and it is right and important that we should. We thank him for the good days and the moments which tell us that it is great to be alive. We tell him about what has gone wrong in our life and expect him to do something about it. We ask so many things from him for ourselves and for others. Before we know it, we can be dangerously near trying to use God for our own purposes; and even if they are honourable purposes we have got the wrong end of the stick. The sense of the 'awesome' has disappeared; we have turned worship and our relationship with God upside down.

It is, of course, easy to see other people trying to use God for their own purposes. It was hard not to be cynical when Saddam Hussain donned the mantle of the devout Moslem, appealing to his people to sacrifice themselves in a 'holy war' against the infidels. Yes, easy to see in other people, but much more difficult to face the troubling thought that we may make the same mistake. It was hard, indeed for many people it was unpatriotic, once our own forces were in the Gulf, not to assume that our motives and that of our allies were pure, and that we could confidently assume that God was on our side. But we gather for worship, not to assure ourselves that God is on our side nor to tell him what we expect him to do, but to bow before the mystery of his presence, to put ourselves at his disposal and to pray that his will may be done in and through us. That is why what is central to worship may be summed up in one word –'adoration' – that response to God which comes naturally and inevitably out of that sense of awe and wonder which entered Jacob's life that night at Bethel.

I was travelling one evening with one of my daughters across the Kingston Bridge over the Clyde in Glasgow, when suddenly she said 'look'. There it was: a clear evening sky, the dark outline of silent cranes, ships and distant hills etched against the blazing brightness of the sun slowly setting in its halo of orange, red and purple. It was one of those moments when nothing needs to be said, when nothing adequate *can* be said. You know you are in the presence of something much bigger and more wonderful than yourself. It makes you feel small and humble, yet curiously glad to be alive, filled with a sense of wonder and awe. That is what lies at the heart of all true worship. That is why hymns and prayers of adoration must come first in every act of worship, before ever we confess our sins or ask God for anything.

O worship the King all-glorious above,
O gratefully sing his power and his love,

Our Shield and Defender, the Ancient of Days,
Pavilioned in splendour, and girded with praise.

O tell of his might, O sing of his grace,
Whose robe is the light, whose canopy space.
His chariots of wrath the deep thunder-clouds form,
And dark is his path on the wings of the storm.

~ Hymn 35, vv 1-2 (*Church Hymnary,* Third Edition) ~

This is the moment when we are lifted out of ourselves to look at life in the light of the mystery and wonder of God. It is when we worship God, not because of the things he gives us, but simply because of who he is, the God whose greatest gift to us is the gift of himself as he comes to us in Jesus.

As the Shorter Catechism puts it: 'Man's chief end is to glorify God and to enjoy him for ever'; to glorify God just because he is God, and to see ourselves in the light of that larger vision of one whose majesty and greatness can never be fully grasped in any mere words of ours. That is why we need the artist as well as the preacher, the poet as well as the teacher, sound, light and colour as well as words, the drama, the action of the sacraments, breaking of bread and sharing of wine, and what we so often neglect – silence. We need them all, so that here we may be touched by a sense of worship and go from this place able to say with Jacob: *'How awesome is this place! This is none other than the house of God; it is the gateway to heaven.'*

That means, of course, placing the whole of life in a new perspective. It is a perspective beautifully and simply put in that delightful book, *Mister God. This is Anna.* As the author describes it: 'It is simply the ability to move out of "I am the centre of all things" and to let something or someone else take over. And as for Anna, she simply moved out and let Mister God move in.' That

23

was what Jacob was discovering that night at Bethel. It means taking with us into our daily lives a vision of the mystery of the love of God which will haunt us and refuse to allow us to be content to live within the limited horizons of our own selfish ambitions and desires. It means taking with us the challenge to share with others the mystery of the love of God which here in worship we celebrate. It was that vision and that mystery which touched Jacob's life one night at Bethel. It was the beginning of the end of the old Jacob, who thought that life and other people only existed to ensure that he made it to the top. He knew he was no longer the centre of things. He had to move out and let God move in: and this is never easy. It is not merely a question of learning to shout 'Hallelujah' or 'Jesus saves' or finding a warm glow in singing familiar choruses. That can be just as much a self-centred experience as any denial of God. To let God move in means letting other people move in. It means responding to the needs of others in the community and in the wider world which is God's world. It means taking on board a commitment which not even a lifetime of service can exhaust.

Jacob had painful experiences ahead. There was much that he could only learn the hard way. But that night was for him the beginning. Worship offers us again and again just such a beginning, a beginning which sets us on the road which leads towards that end when God's purposes for our lives and for his world will find their fulfilment. As St Paul puts it:

At present we see only puzzling reflections in a mirror, but one day we shall see face to face. My knowledge now is partial; then it will be whole, like God's knowledge of me.

~ 1 Corinthians 13:12 ~

But we do see now, however dimly, as we gather in worship to celebrate the mystery of God's goodness to and love for each one of us. Our feet are on the road to that complete knowledge of God which will one day be ours. Or to change the picture which Paul uses: worship is like a window, a window through which the mysterious light of God's presence comes to shine into our lives, a window through which we can look out to catch a glimpse of a richer, and more challenging deeper life than we could otherwise know. That is the life which alone gives meaning to our life. It is the life to which God is calling us whenever we gather for worship.

What's in a Name?

Moses said to God, 'If I come to the Israelites and tell them that the God of their forefathers has sent me to them, and they ask me his name, what am I to say to them?' God answered, 'I am that I am. Tell them that I am has sent you to them'.

~ Exodus 3:13-14 ~

WHAT'S in a name? 'God of a Hundred Names' is the title of a collection of prayers drawn from people of many different lands and many different faiths; as if to say, what does it matter what we call God, as long as we believe in that great reality which lies beyond our lives and gives meaning to them. Perhaps Moses could have saved himself, and God, a lot of trouble if only he could have settled for that, and stopped worrying about such a trivial matter as God's name. But he couldn't. Moses had his problems, some of them real, some of them no doubt imaginary – and the more he thought about them the more daunting they seemed to be. Called by God to be the Fidel Castro of ancient Israel, Moses must have known that his revolutionary credentials were not above suspicion. He had been brought up as the favoured son of the oppressive regime he was now committed to challenge. He had spent years in comfortable exile, cut off from his enslaved fellow countrymen. Now he was back, back to organise these slaves, to prepare them for a freedom march.

Small wonder that he was apprehensive. He could see all kinds

26

of difficulties looming ahead. Suppose he were to be questioned about his authority, about his right to lead the freedom march – what was he to say? He had no revolutionary council to back him up, no party manifesto to distribute among the workers. His sole platform … 'the God of your forefathers has sent me to you'. It didn't sound very convincing. He imagines the retort: 'The God of our forefathers? What God? …. What is his name?' For the Old Testament a name is not merely a convenient label, it is a pointer to a person's character, just as our nicknames so very often are. Call a person a 'moaning Minnie' and you are saying something about the kind of person he or she is. What is his name? Ask that question about God and you are asking what this God is like, what is his real character, what can we know about him? It is as if you are asking for a creed: such a creed was not to be God's gift to Moses.

'And God said to Moses, "I am that I am" [or perhaps better "I will be who I will be"]. *Tell them I am* [or I will be] *has sent you to them'* (Exodus 3:14). In many ways these are puzzling words. There is little doubt that they are trying to tell us something about why the Hebrews knew God by the name 'Yahweh' (mistranslated Jehovah in the Authorised Version, usually rendered in modern translations as 'LORD'). They are linking that name with the verb 'to be' or 'to become' or 'to happen'. But beyond that, all is specu-lation. The last word has not and probably never will be spoken concerning this verse.

It is certainly possible to read all kinds of things into these words. Someone once said to me that they left him with the picture of a somewhat pompous God standing on his dignity and saying to Moses: 'Don't ask silly questions; if you do, you will only get a silly answer!' So is Moses being given the brush off by God? I don't think that is the intention of this story. Let me suggest to you that the words 'I will be who I will be' are meant to be both an answer and a refusal to give an answer to Moses' question.

Notice first what these words *don't* say. They don't say, 'I will be what you want me to be'. Some years ago there was published a collection of essays entitled *The God I Want*. The essays tell us a great deal about the writers, about their religious upbringing or lack of it, about their own theological stance, radical or conservative. It is full of fascinating autobiographical reflections, but what does it say about God? One of the most interesting contributions in it is by Antony Burgess, and it consists of a Platonic type dialogue between 'Antony' and 'Burgess'. Speak to yourself long enough and you will certainly get 'the God you want'.

I once went into a bank to cash a cheque given to me by a church treasurer. It was Monday morning. I was wearing a sports jacket and flannels, and flaunting a somewhat loud tie. He looked at the cheque; he looked at me. 'Are you a minister?' he said. Once the great confession had been made, he launched into telling me all the reasons why he no longer went to church. He didn't like some of the people who went. The sermons often meant nothing to him. He was happier on the golf course on a Sunday morning. He still of course sent the kids to Sunday School. 'But don't misunderstand me,' he said, 'I still believe in God. I'm a keen gardener. I sow seeds, the seeds send up green shoots, the shoots grow into flowers or vegetables. I look at it and think it can't be an accident, there must be "someone somewhere".' No doubt he was happy enough with that vague 'someone somewhere'; perhaps it was a comforting religious insurance policy. That was the God he wanted. The God, however, who comes to us through the witness of the Bible, might often be more truly described as the God we do not want!

The Hebrew slaves in Egypt, to whom Moses was sent, wanted freedom. They got it. This is God's gift to you, said Moses, a gift they were challenged to accept. What they did not anticipate was that this God who led them to freedom was the same God who would face them with uncompromising demands, a God who would make life exceedingly uncomfortable for them when they failed to respond to these demands, a God who would in the end be prepared to take away the freedom he had given.

I am the LORD your God who brought you out of Egypt, out of the land of slavery .... You must not .... You must ....

~ Exodus 20:2ff ~

Often we seem to want only a God who will be a problem solver, who will help us neatly to fit together the jagged pieces of our lives and of the puzzling world in which we live. One of the contributors to *The God I Want* declares that the only god he could worship would be a god who came up with an answer to the problem of evil and suffering, and came up with it quickly. If that is the God we want, a 'neat answer' God, then the Bible is liable to be disappointing. It often leaves us with a God who forces people to ask questions, questions which lead them to protest because what they know of this God must rule out many of the easy answers to the deepest mysteries of life.

Think of the book of Job. It was Job's friends, you remember, who had all the correct religious answers when Job was on the receiving end of appalling, and what to him was meaningless, suffering. Yet the book ends ironically by declaring that the friends had got it wrong, that they had not spoken as they ought to have spoken about God; while Job who had screamed curses at God and rejected all the facile answers which did not square with his experience, finds himself facing a God, majestic and mysterious beyond his imagining, yet a God who accepts him and sees in his protests and his agonising questions the searching of faith.

Job's friends were sure of the God they wanted; and if Job's experience did not fit into what they believed about that God, so

29

much the worse for Job. The trouble with 'the God I want' is that this is inevitably to some extent a God cut down to the size of my own ability to imagine or to recognise; a God often cramped within beliefs we have been taught, but have never put to the test. Commenting on the way in which the statement 'outside the church there is no salvation' has sometimes been understood by fellow Roman Catholics, a Roman Catholic writer says: 'The quaint implication that God is somehow first and foremost a Roman Catholic, may appeal to God's sense of humour, if to nothing else .... '

We can only trust that God has a sense of humour. He badly needs it if only to handle some of those who most passionately and publicly declare their total devotion to him. I once overheard a student say to another student, 'your Jesus is not my Jesus'. He then proceeded in all the arrogance of humility to demonstrate how his Jesus was the only possible true understanding of Jesus, and his attitude to the Bible the only one which could sustain a meaningful faith. That student told me a lot about the God he wanted and, no doubt for a variety of reasons, needed, but very little about the God who says to Moses: 'I will be who I will be'. That God, as he listened, must have either laughed or cried.

Tell us what is God's name, said the people to Moses; and in reply God says to Moses, 'I will be who I will be'. I suggested that in these words we can find both an answer and a refusal to give an answer to the people's question. So far we have been thinking about what these words don't say, the answer they refuse to give, but at another level they were an answer to the people's need to know about God. They say one thing loud and clear. This is a God who is present with Moses in all his doubts, present with an enslaved people in their pain, suffering and questioning; and this is a God who will be present whatever may happen. 'I will be ... I will be with you': this is a promise which runs like a golden thread through the Bible. The answer is a promise, a promise which is a call to trust, to take the risk of stepping out into the unknown future with many questions unanswered and unanswerable, but with one unshakeable certainty that in that future God will be there. The answer is the promise of God's presence, but beyond that these words refuse to go. How God's presence will come to his people, what form it will take in the future, the comfort and the challenge it will bring, only the future will unfold. God is there to be discovered and rediscovered, experienced and re-experienced in the ever changing patterns of life. 'I will be who I will be' … the door is closed on any neatly labelled fossil of a God, but the door is opened to a life of commitment and growing faith in an ever active God who will always remain true to himself.

It is said that when a Jew does not have a ready answer to a question, he tells a story. Here is one such traditional Jewish story. It is about the town of Sodom which, along with its twin city of Gomorrah, had a certain reputation for notoriety in the Old Testament. In all good and edifying stories, of course, evil is never left entirely unchallenged. One of the Just Men, so this story goes, came to Sodom determined to save its inhabitants from sin and punishment. Night and day he walked its streets and markets preaching against greed and theft, falsehood and indifference. At first people listened and smiled ironically. Then they stopped listening; he no longer even amused them. The killers went on killing, the wise kept silent, as if there were no Just Man in their midst. One day a child, moved by compassion for the unfortunate preacher, approached him with these words:

'Poor stranger, you shout, you expend yourself body and soul; don't you see that it is hopeless?'
   'Yes I see,' answered the Just Man.
   'Then why do you go on?'
   'I'll tell you why. In the beginning I thought I could change

31

people. Today I know I can't. If I still shout today, if I still scream,
it is to prevent people from ultimately changing me.'

That story is a defiant affirmation of human integrity, of a man
who refused to allow himself to become other than he was: but it is
also a parable of the God who says to Moses, 'I will be who I will
be', a parable of the God who keeps coming to us, even when it
seems hopeless and people pay no heed. He keeps coming
because he can do no other, coming in ways that may often surprise us.

'I will be who I will be', not 'I will be who you want me to
be.' Perhaps at no time do we need to be more forcibly reminded of
this than at the season of Advent. It is part of the blindness which
surrounds our approach to Christmas that we have so wrapped up
the Christ event in tinselled religiosity that it gives only the God we
want – a heart-warming, reassuring God who causes no offence
and asks for no commitment except an annual orgy of nostalgic
sentimentality; the God we can switch off when we switch off the
Christmas lights.

Advent is not about the God we want. It takes us to the God
who challenges many of the values upon which we, and the society
in which we live, try to build our lives. This is the God who in the
words of the Magnificat:

scatters the proud in the imagination of their hearts,
puts down the might from their thrones ...
exalts those of low degree ...
fills the hungry with good things ...
sends the rich empty away ....

This is the God in whom we are rightly invited to rejoice, but
only when like him we are prepared to set aside all pretence to

self importance and share in the pain and the joy, the needs and the hopes of others.

Light looked down and saw darkness ....
  'I will go there,' said LIGHT;
Peace looked down and saw war ....
  'I will go there,' said PEACE;
Love looked down and saw hatred ....
  'I will go there,' said LOVE;
So he, the Light of life, the Prince of Peace, the King of Love,
  came down and crept in beside us.

This is God who meets us in the story which runs from Moses to Bethlehem and beyond, the God who says 'I will be who I will be', the God who reveals to us who he is unchangeably in Jesus.

Vision and Reality

… they shall beat their swords into ploughshares,
and their spears into pruning hooks;
nation shall not lift up sword against nation
neither shall they learn war any more.

~ Isaiah 2:4, RSV ~

THESE are familiar words. They appear in the message of two of the prophets of Israel, Isaiah and Micah, two men closely associated with a city, the city of Jerusalem, some 700 years before the beginning of the Christian era. The words appear in the middle of a passage which might have been produced by the Public Relations Department of the Jerusalem City Council. Jerusalem, it is claimed, will one day be the cultural and the religious centre of world:

Many nations will stream towards it ….

to be taught by the God of Israel, to walk in his paths and to follow a vision of a world at peace, with swords beaten into ploughshares and spears into pruning hooks. It was a vision which must have found an echo in the hearts of many people in Israel itself. They knew only too well the grim reality of war: villages pillaged, fields left untilled, vineyards untended because of the threat or the presence of an invading army. It is a vision to which many people then, and now, would gladly say 'Amen'.

Not so familiar perhaps are the words of a later prophet Joel, words which seem directly to contradict this vision. No longer an invitation to the nations to follow a vision of a world at peace, but a call to arms:

Prepare war, stir up the mighty men .... Beat your ploughshares into swords, and your pruning hooks into spears; let the weak say, 'I am a warrior'.

~ Joel 3:9-10, RSV ~

Is this just another example of these infuriating contradictions we find in the Bible? Is Joel saying to us that there is no harm in having visions, but they can never be a substitute for hard-headed realism? We live in a world where force must be met with force, where there is no excuse for sentimental weakness. Do these two passages simply highlight the clash between vision and reality which still haunts us; the clash between those who demonstrated against the first Trident submarine sailing into Faslane under the banner 'Turn Trident into scrap'; and those who believe that we need Trident and other nuclear weapons because there is no substitute for military preparedness in the uncertain world in which we live? Must we then side either with the dreamers of visions or the clear-eyed realists?

No, there is more to it than that. When Isaiah points his people towards a vision of a world at peace, he is not encouraging them to dream idle dreams or to indulge in private fantasies to keep them cheerful when the going is rough; he is calling them to a new way of life. The passage ends with the words:

Come, people of Israel,
    let us walk in the light of the LORD.

~ Isaiah 2:5 ~

35

A prophet's vision is never a way of escape from the harsh realities of life; it is always a challenge, a challenge to people to redirect their lives, to live in the light of something which can enlarge and enrich their lives and the lives of others, if only they are prepared to face the cost of so doing. Isaiah's vision was a recognition of present failure and a call to reach out beyond present failures to a new life which would celebrate God's values. The present failures were there in Isaiah's day; there for everyone to see if only they had eyes to see them. This Jerusalem, says the prophet, is a city awash with silver and gold, a city of affluence and prestige developments; and a city of 'bleeding wounds', a city of social deprivation for many, where those most in need, the fatherless, the widow and the poor, struggled merely to survive. It is disturbingly, or is it just acceptably familiar?

A few days before Christmas one of our daily newspapers carried a full page colour advert for 'The Best of Scotland', commending, no doubt with some justification, the merits of a particular brand of whisky. On the opposite page in chilling black and white there was a picture of the huddled figures in a cardboard city, homeless, some of them Scots, some of them mentally inadequate, discharged into the community without the needed provision of continuing community care. What would give them 'The Best of Scotland'?

You can have the vision, says the prophet, but there is a price to be paid:

- … the price of being prepared to walk in God's ways, working for a society which will honour 'Justice and Righteousness' instead of privilege and profit;
- … the price of caring for other people, instead of believing that making it to the top yourself is the only thing which matters; the price of replacing anger and hatred with patience and love;

- ... the price of being prepared to work for a society and a community of nations free from the scourge of war, because they are free from the prejudices, the injustices, the fears and inequalities which lead to conflict.

To walk in the way of the Lord was Isaiah's call to heal the divisions in personal relationships and in the life of the community in which he lived. The call is still the same. There is a price to be paid for such a vision.

What of that other prophet, Joel, with his call to the nations to prepare for war? When he says *'beat your ploughshares into swords and your pruning hooks into spears'*, he is not merely being a hard-headed realist. He is issuing a warning. Prepare for war, he says; there will perhaps be times when you have no alternative, but remember there is a bitter harvest to be reaped, a 'land steeped in blood'. Prepare for war, but do not glory in it. To be caught up in the violence of war is to enter the valley of judgement and to be brought face to face with the dire consequences of your decisions and your actions. Yes, Joel is a realist, a hard-headed realist, convinced that not to walk in the light of the Lord is to be engulfed in coming darkness.

We see that darkness daily on our television screens. The devastated, gaping towns, the broken families, the mangled bodies, the despair wracked faces of homeless people in what was once Yugoslavia. We saw it in Somalia where desperately needed food lay undistributed or was looted, because rival factions would rather fight each other than co-operate to save millions who have died or are dying of starvation. We have seen it in the vicious inter-tribal rivalry in Rwanda with its appalling consequences for millions of frightened people. In our own country we see the price that had to be paid in the names inscribed in the countless war memorials throughout our land.

Two prophets, Isaiah and Joel, place before us a choice, a choice which has never been more urgent; to beat our swords into ploughshares or our ploughshares into swords. Either way – there is a price to be paid.

From two prophets who speak to us across the centuries, we turn to two Christians of today: one from China, one from present day Israel. In a small community not far from the city of Hangzhou there is a remarkable man, Elder Lu. He was brought up in a Christian home, but, as he puts it, 'lost his way'. During the cultural revolution he was an active member of the Communist Party. He knew how to deal with any 'dissidents' who did not enthusiastically embrace the thoughts of Chairman Mao. Violence, bullying and fear were the weapons with which to control or eliminate the enemies of the people. One day in 1976 his wife was seriously injured in a fall. He found himself face to face with something which no amount of violence could change and that nothing in the power he wielded over other people could solve. His sister came to him to speak of another kind of power, the healing power of the love of God which comes to us in Jesus. She suggested that they should pray that this power would heal his wife. At first he was sceptical, but since he saw no other solution he began to pray. Gradually healing came to his wife. He vowed to rededicate his life to Jesus. There was a price to be paid, in terms of his relationship to the Party and former comrades. In 1980 he began to meet with five other people in his home to study the Bible and to pray. Today, while holding down a responsible job in a civil engineering company, he acts as part time pastor to a congregation of 800 in his own town, a congregation which has had to move five times since 1985 because of growing numbers. Last year eighty people were baptised. Every Sunday there are three services – morning, afternoon and evening – all of them packed. Here is a man who had set aside the sword, the violence, the bullying, the threats, and was planting the seeds of a new kind of life which was bearing fruit in the lives of many other people.

Let us turn now to the city of Isaiah, the city of Jerusalem, the Jerusalem of the present day. In the midst of the crisis in relationships between Palestinians and Jews consequent upon Saddam Hussain's invasion of Kuwait, and in the shadow of impending war in the Gulf, Bishop Kafiti, the Anglican Bishop of Jerusalem, himself a Palestinian, expressed the hope that out of the present turmoil would come 'a transformation into a new life, lived in faithfulness to God, where hatred is replaced by love, violence by dialogue, condemnation by forgiveness, self-centredness by sharing, and war by peace'. That is a hope still struggling to be born, a hope that surely we all share. There is, however, little point in sharing it unless we face the challenge it brings. Are we prepared in our relationship with other people to practise forgiveness and sharing, instead of condemnation and self-centredness? Do we accept that hatred and violence can never be substitutes for love and dialogue? Are we prepared to remind ourselves and our leaders that war is no substitute for the patient search for peace?

Only then can we claim to be people with a vision, prepared to look at ourselves, at our church, at our community in the light of that vision which in its full glory comes to us in Jesus. It is easier and more comfortable not to look. It is harder and more disturbing to look because it means there is a way for each of us to walk, a way which took Jesus to the cross. Where vision and reality walk hand in hand, there is always a price to be paid.

Whither the Church?

IN Isaiah 40 we read these words:

Jacob, why do you complain,
and you, Israel, why do you say,
'My lot is hidden from the LORD,
my cause goes unheeded by my God'?   ~ Isaiah 40:27 ~

Here is a prophet who had his ear to the ground, who had been listening to what other people were saying. What he heard were words of bitterness and disillusionment. He knew what his fellow Jews were experiencing. He was with them in exile in Babylon. Their distant homeland was in the hands of occupation troops. Their world had collapsed. Everything which had given them security in the past, all the outward signs of their faith – the land God had given them, the temple in Jerusalem where God dwelt in their midst, that holy city which they confidently believed could never be destroyed – all was gone. They had been thrown out into a cold and cruel world where their faith was derided or regarded as irrelevant. They found it hard to come to terms with what had happened. No wonder they complained. Either God no longer cared what happened to them, or he was powerless to do anything about it. They wanted to go back, back to the comfort and security they had once known. The present was too confusing and perplexing. Faith was no longer an accepted or an easy option.

There are those in the church who seem to wish to respond to the world in which God has placed us today in much the same way. Let's return, they say, to that time when in former generations the Kirk was at the centre of the life of Scotland, its role clear and recognised by all in the community. Why can't we go back to the Reformation or to the church as it was when that memorable General Assembly met here in Glasgow in 1638, a few months after the signing of the National Covenant? Or should we not go back further still and seek to recreate today the life and worship of the church in New Testament times? Is this to be the answer for Christian discipleship today in a society in which the church is marginalised, where in some areas of our cities less than five per cent of the population have any church connection, and where much of the structure of church life and the forms of worship we have inherited no longer ring bells for many of our young people, not least those brought up in Christian homes? I think not. Not all our longings or our prayers can turn the clock back. We cannot retreat to, or seek to hide in, the past, however rich a heritage that past may be. The once powerful slogans of yesterday are not the answer to the crying needs of today. To think of the church and its mission in such terms is close to regarding the church as a fossil, attractive perhaps, but still a dead fossil instead of a living organism, capable of changing and adapting to its God-given environment while retaining its essential identity.

Let us listen again to this prophet responding to those words of bitterness and disillusionment which he heard in his day. He comes to his fellow exiles to say to them – and I wonder whether they were disappointed when they heard it – there is nothing new I have to say to you, no new picture of God to offer to you, no newly discovered spiritual pain-killer to help you to cope with your troubles. I can offer you nothing but what you already know or ought to know.

Do you not know, have you not heard?
The LORD, the eternal God,
creator of earth's farthest bounds,
does not grow weary or grow faint;
his understanding cannot be fathomed.

~ Isaiah 40:28 ~

Do you not know? .... Were you not told long ago? .... Have you not heard? In question after question this prophet takes them back; but not back to the securities of the past for which they longed, not back to the old pattern of life or the forms of worship with which they had been familiar. He takes them back instead to the God of their past, the God who, he claims, is still the God of their present. This is the God 'creator of earth's farthest bounds' who has the whole world, even Babylon, in his hands; the God who is with them in exile, sharing their bitterness and disappointment, and speaking to them through it. You are bitter and confused, he claims, not because the world in which you are placed is too cold and cruel, too perplexing and puzzling for you to handle. You are bitter and confused because you have lost hold on your vision of God. Your picture of God is too limited, your thoughts about him too mean. And this is the point to which we must always return – to the God who spoke to his people in the past, calling them to a discipleship meaningful in their day, to the God who would speak to us now, calling us to a discipleship meaningful in our day.

Not that this will bring us any easy comfort or slick answers. We may join enthusiastically in singing the Magnificat, affirming our faith in a God who *'has stretched out his mighty arm and scattered the proud with all their plans. He has brought down the mighty from their thrones and lifted up the lowly ....'* (Luke 1:51-52).

We may rejoice when we see this happening elsewhere, when

42

once proud and powerful regimes in Eastern Europe collapse. Do we not, however, often continue to live as if this was not the God we worship; aligning ourselves with the mighty and the proud and not with the lowly and the poor, devoting much of our time, energy and resources to defending our privileges, manning the barricades of our inherited power structures in church and society?

We confess our faith in the Christ who *'is himself our peace. Gentiles and Jews, he has made the two one, and in his own body of flesh and blood has broken down the barrier of enmity which separated them ... so as to create out of the two a single new humanity in himself, thereby making peace'* (Ephesians 2:14-15). But we are far from celebrating that single new humanity in the church. We still find it impossible or unimportant to break down the barriers which separate us even from our own brothers and sisters in Christ.

Is it surprising that we face a credibility gap? I am not thinking here of that gap which those outside the church often see only too clearly between what we profess to believe and what we are. That is real enough. I am thinking rather of the credibility gap which is there at the centre of our own thinking and living. We claim so much, but so little of it disturbs or renews our lives.

Small wonder then that the prophet's first word to his embittered and confused fellow exiles is to challenge them to look back, not nostalgically to what they thought of as the good old days, but back to the resources which were there in the faith they once claimed to profess, back to the God who they thought had forsaken them. There is no use pretending that we are spiritually bankrupt, if we never draw on the capital we have been given.

If the prophet's first word is a call to look back, his second word, surprisingly, is 'don't look back'. This is the word of the Lord, he says:

Stop dwelling on past events
and brooding over days gone by.
I am about to do something new;
this moment it will unfold.
Can you not perceive it?

~ Isaiah 43:18-19 ~

The prophet was well aware of the danger that his people would be blind to the new thing God was doing in their midst, because they were prisoners of their past. It is all too easy to allow ourselves to become prisoners of our past, particularly if our past is marked by achievement and success, as the history of the church to which we belong has so often been. But we dare not become so trapped, for the church is not only the church of the past, but the church of the present and the future.

We can, of course, clearly see how other people can be the prisoners of their past. Face to face with the disturbingly new in Jesus, and being offered the truth which would set them free, many of the most devout Jews took refuge in their deep-seated conviction: '*We are Abraham's descendants .... Abraham is our father*' (John 8:33,39). They were right so to claim. They were God's people, privileged and enriched by a tradition of faith which went back to their pilgrim forefather Abraham. They were, however, so set and secure in traditional ways of thinking and living which alone for them contained the reality of God, that they found it impossible to see God's new way, there in their midst in Jesus. We look at them, we think how blind, how tragic, what a missed opportunity; but we seldom realise that that is often where we are in the church, blind to the purposes and presence of God in our midst, not because we live in a godless and confusing world, but because we have locked ourselves into patterns of church life and witness which were a faithful and creative response to God in the past, but which are no longer adequate for the rapidly changing world in which God has placed us today. It is as if we have drawn a map of God's world and marked the place of the church in it. We have plotted exactly where we expect God to be and noted the routes he takes. Inevitably, of course, he walks along our own 'Church Road'. But increasingly we are being forced to question whether the map we have drawn is adequate.

Recently an attempt to deliver a washing machine to our house ran into trouble, and took much longer than it should have taken, because the street in which we now live was not on the delivery driver's map. The street, however, does exist; although it wasn't on that map, we do live there. And God *is* out there, even if we are using an out-of-date map.

We are not called to remain as we are or where we are, nor to retreat into the past. We are called to go out with the gospel into our world, knowing that God is there before us. He is there sharing the honest questions, the frustration, the confusion, the pain and the longings of people today. Only when we learn such sharing shall new life come to us from the God who is there, the God who has always been there.

In light of recent events in the Soviet Union and other Eastern European countries, the Soviet Foreign Minister, E. Shevarnadze, spoke of the dilemma which had long faced the Soviet leadership:

> ... *whether to prefer the anxiety of someone who knows the truth or the tranquillity of those who ignore it. Truth, he claimed, is better: without truth there can be no future.*

For too long many of us have seen the church as a haven of rest and tranquillity in a stormy world, a church existing to give us assurance and comfort. Yes, there is such assurance and comfort, but it can only be the assurance and comfort of pilgrims and fellow travellers, not of those desperately manning the barricades of their own shrinking stockades. To travel together is to be open to change, to sharing new experiences. To grasp the new thing to which God is calling us today is to become unsettled and vulnerable. I wonder why we ever thought it could be otherwise?

In Paul's day the barriers were coming down: Jews and Gentiles, slaves and free, men and women becoming one in the church, sign of that one new humanity in Christ. But let us never forget how this happened. It was not because people sat down together and politely agreed to differ. It was not because they signed the same credal statement or because they had the same theology of ministry or of the church. It was because Christ *'made the two one ... in his own body of flesh and blood ...* [because he reconciled] *the two in a single body ... <u>through the cross,</u> by which he killed the enmity'* (Ephesians 2:14,16). As Michael Taylor, Director of Christian Aid, once put it: 'there is no way of Christian hope for the church or for the world ... which goes round the cross; it must go through the cross.' But that means death, before there can be resurrection, not merely for other churches or for other people – but for us.

As we enter the last rapidly changing decade of this century, we do not know how much of our present pattern of church life can carry us into the next century. There are serious question marks being placed against much of it. But this we do know:

- we are in the hands of the same God who journeyed with his people in the past;
- it is the same Jesus who is asking us to lay aside our blinding securities so that we may be open to his presence and to his challenge;
- and it is the same Spirit who will be present to lead and to strengthen us for the demands of today and tomorrow.

To this God, Father, Son and Holy Spirit be ascribed all glory and honour now and forever .... Amen.

[Moderatorial Sermon – Glasgow Cathedral, 20 May 1990.]

Love Unchanging

Can a woman forget the infant at her breast,
or a mother the child of her womb?
But should even these forget,
I shall never forget you.

~ Isaiah 49:15 ~

SHE was a very ordinary, down-to-earth woman from the East end of Glasgow. Her son was standing trial at the high court for a particularly vicious and brutal assault. Before the trial began she vehemently protested his innocence to anyone prepared to listen. My Jimmy would never have done a thing like that, she said. As the trial progressed and the evidence became more and more damning, Jimmy changed his plea to guilty and was sentenced to a lengthy term in prison. Asked by the reporter of a local paper what her reaction was, she said, 'He's still my son; he is and always will be part of me'. There was a mother speaking of the relationship which bound her to her child, a relationship which she believed could never be broken no matter what happened to her son, no matter what he had done.

The Old Testament is the story of a relationship between God and a people, a relationship which we often describe by the word 'covenant', though the Old Testament itself employs many different pictures to describe it. It was a relationship often under strain, a relationship which the people sometimes thought had snapped.

We hear them saying so:

> ... *Zion says, 'The LORD has forsaken me;*
> *my LORD has forgotten me'.*

> ~ Isaiah 49:14 ~

It is small wonder that people were giving voice to such thoughts. These were people who had once lived comfortably and securely in the shadow of the temple in Jerusalem. God was in his heaven and all was right in their little world. The God who ruled the world was there in their midst, guaranteeing that Jerusalem, the holy city, would ride serenely through the storms of political upheavals and pagan threats. Other cities might perish, but never this city:

> *God is in her midst; she will not be overthrown,*
> *and at the break of day he will help her.*
> *Nations are in tumult, kingdoms overturned;*
> *when he thunders, the earth melts.*
> *The LORD of Hosts is with us;*
> *the God of Jacob is our fortress.*

> ~ Psalm 46:5-7 ~

So they sang as they gathered for worship; but it all went horribly wrong. The city was sacked, the temple became a charred ruin. They were in exile, cut off from what previously had been for them the means of grace. No wonder they thought they had been 'forsaken' and 'forgotten' by the God they once worshipped. The relationship with God in which they had once rejoiced and upon which they had depended to see them safely through life was in tatters. They were in trouble and God had let them down. But if that were true, wouldn't that have been a strange kind of relationship? Isn't that a relationship not worth tuppence compared with that of a mother who sees her son in trouble, confessing to a sordid crime, and says through her tears, 'He's still my son, he is and always will be part of me'? Argue as these people argued and you are saying that God is much less dependable, much less loving than that mother. Interestingly the prophet argues the opposite way:

> *But Zion says,*
> *'The LORD has forsaken me;*
> *my LORD has forgotten me'.*
> *Can a woman forget the infant at her breast,*
> *or a mother the child of her womb?*
> *But should even these forget,*
> *I shall never forget you.*
>
> ~ Isaiah 49:14-15 ~

Take the strongest of human relationships you can imagine, says the prophet to his despairing people, and be assured that the relationship which binds God to you and you to God is stronger still. It is as if God is saying to them, 'You are still my people; you are and always will be part of me', no matter what changes you may have to face, no matter how despondent or inadequate you feel. It is the type of argument that Jesus used more than once. Take a situation drawn from human life, take the best you can see in human relationships, and then say 'how much more must that be true of God' (cf Luke 11:11-13).

But what evidence is there that that is true? The evidence is there in our hands and on our lips every time we share in the Sacrament of the Lord's Supper. It takes us back to the last of the many meals Jesus must have shared with his disciples.

The disciples had been with Jesus for the better part of three years. They were the people who knew Jesus best. They had heard his teaching to the crowds and had listened as he patiently explained to them its deepest meaning. They had seen his acts of healing and wondered at his concern for the unloved and the loveless. They had come to believe that in a strange and unique way God was present with them in this man Jesus. And yet, as they gathered that night they were afraid and confused:

- Jesus had been talking about suffering and dying, and that didn't make sense, even though he had caused offence to influential people.
- One of them sharing that meal was biding his time till he could slip out into the night to betray Jesus to his enemies.
- Others were arguing about who was going to be greatest in the Kingdom of God. Peter was putting his foot in it again, making passionate promises which Jesus knew he would not be able to keep.

The relationship between Jesus and those who knew him best, we might have thought would have been a relationship of trust and understanding. It was anything but – and Jesus knew it. What could he do, what could he give them which he had not already given? Nothing, but himself. Bread broken – 'this is my body'; wine poured out – 'this is my blood, the blood of the covenant, shed for many'. It is not difficult, is it, to see ourselves mirrored in the disciples who shared that last meal with Jesus?

There are times when we are afraid and confused, when we find it difficult to come to terms with the horrifying and senseless things that happen day by day in what we believe to be God's world, horrifying and senseless things which can sometimes touch our own lives or the lives of those nearest and dearest to us.

There are the promises we have made, promises made to God when publicly we confessed our faith here in church. Have these promises always been kept? You know in your experience, as I do in mine, that they haven't.

There have been the betrayals, the times when we ought to have nailed our colours to the mast as Christians and haven't had the courage to do so.

There are the times when we have failed to understand what the Kingdom of God is all about, and at the top of our agenda has been the need to defend our own reputation, or that of the congregation or the church to which we belong.

As we gather at the Lord's table, we share something of the fears, the failures, the misunderstandings of the disciples as they shared that last meal with Jesus. But we also share something else, a need which is met as we handle the ordinary, common things of bread and wine. Towards the end of his life, Dietrich Bonhoeffer received in his concentration camp on Whit Sunday a small parcel from some friends. In reply he wrote:

> *Such things give me greater joy than I can say. Although I am utterly convinced that nothing can break the bonds between us, I seem to need some outward token and sign to reassure me. In this way material things become the vehicles of spiritual realities. I suppose it is rather like the need felt in all religions for sacraments.*

In face of our fears, failures and misunderstandings, bread and wine answer our need to know that whatever happens to us, however much we continue to hurt him, God, the God who was Israel's refuge and strength, the God who comes to us in Jesus never lets go. He holds us in a relationship which nothing can ever break, not even death itself.

Can a woman forget the infant at her breast,
or a mother the child in her womb?
But should even these forget,
I shall never forget you.

Wanted

This word of the LORD came to me: 'Before I formed you in the womb I chose you, and before you were born I consecrated you; I appointed you a prophet to the nations.'

~ Jeremiah 1:4-5 ~

SEVERAL years ago the BBC screened a fascinating religious documentary series, directed by Richard Eyre, called 'The Long Search'. From the shanty towns of South Africa to the Cathedrals of Europe, from the hippie communes of California to the crowds gathered on the banks of the Ganges, from students in training to become Jewish Rabbis, debating fine points of theology, to the simple devotees of Shintoism at Japanese shrines, we were presented with people throughout the world, in many different ways, following an astonishing variety of customs, reaching out for something or someone beyond themselves, reaching out for what we call God. The series made no attempt to prove or to disprove the truth in different religions: it was content to say 'here is what people do.'

That is how many people think of religion. That is perhaps why we think we should come to church. This is where we reach out to God. The Bible, however, tells a rather different story. Yes, it tells of people reaching out to God, in joy and in hope, in pain and in despair, in certainty and in doubt, but it dares to say to us that behind all our reaching out for God, there is a God who first reaches out for us. It reminds us that we are here members of the church, not because we want God, but because God first wants us.

We were planning a Stewardship visitation in a congregation to which I once belonged. Those who volunteered to visit – the usual few – met to discuss the situations they might face when they began knocking on doors. It was decided to do some role play. One of the elders present, a quiet unassuming man who seldom if ever spoke at Kirk Session meetings, was given a tough assign-ment. You are going to knock on a door, Jimmy. A woman will come to the door and when you say you are from the church the door will be slammed in your face. What are you going to do?

'I'll go back,' said Jimmy, 'and this time I'll make sure I get my foot in the door.'

Once inside, a fairly tense and aggressive conversation was to take place. Jimmy explains why he had come, to be faced with the angry response, 'Why should I give anything to the church. What has it ever given me? Has it given anything to you?'

There was a pause, and then Jimmy said, 'I'll tell you what it has given me; it has made me feel wanted'.

That was what Jeremiah discovered one day. We don't know when or where or how it happened, but he suddenly knew he was wanted, wanted by God. '*Before I formed you in the womb I chose you ....*' It was as if everything in his life up to that moment came together when he heard God saying to him, 'I want you'.

I want you ... and I want you just as you are. Did you notice Jeremiah's response? To be wanted by God, surely that would immediately bring forth a sense of pride and of enthusiasm. Not at all –

'*Ah! Lord God,*' *I answered, '*I am not skilled in speaking; I am too young.*'

It is as if Jeremiah is saying to God, you must be making a

mistake, you've come to the wrong person; there are a lot of other people far more experienced, far more gifted than I am. Why me? Jeremiah wasn't the first – or the last – person to respond to God in this way. Have you ever noticed how often it happens like this in the Bible story. Remember Moses called by God to lead his people out of slavery into freedom, and making excuse after excuse to avoid the call: 'what am I to say to them? … they will never believe me or listen to what I say … I am not a fluent speaker.' And the picture which the book of Exodus leaves us with is of God sitting patiently as excuse after excuse comes pouring out, answering each one of them, and in the end saying to Moses, 'I know all that, but I don't make mistakes, it's you I want, just as you are'. So with Jeremiah; he may plead that there are far more experienced, far more gifted people whom God might or ought to have chosen, but God in reply brushes this plea aside:

> *'Do not plead that you are too young; for you are to go to whatever people I send you, and say whatever I tell you to say. Fear none of them, for I shall be with to keep you safe.'*
>
> ~ Jeremiah 1:7-8 ~

She had had a bad, tiring morning. As she got on the bus in central Glasgow, she was carrying two heavy, well-filled shopping bags in one hand, and with the other she was dragging along behind her a small child, a small child who was equally tired and cross. They struggled on to the bus, and as the child was pushed on to a seat the woman said, 'You sit there and be quiet, or I'll smack you'.

There was silence for a while, then a small voice piped up, 'Mummy, do you love me?'

'Yes,' came the reply, 'yes, when you are good.'

It's worth remembering that Jesus never said anything like that. He didn't approach people and say, 'If you are good enough you

can be my disciple'. He didn't go round with a notebook pencilling
in the good qualities and the defects which people had, saying to
some 'You'll do' and to others 'Sorry, you will never make it. He
walked along the shore of a lake, saw a group of fishermen working at their nets and said, 'Come ... I want you'. And he said it to
some strange people. That was what shocked some of the most
respectable, deeply religious, God-fearing folk of his day. Jesus
often spoke to and went into the homes of people in whose company
they would have shuddered to be seen, and he assured such people
that God loved and wanted them, in spite of their faults and failings
which others so loudly condemned.

We have a saying that 'Love is blind'. Nothing is further from
the truth, not where real love is concerned. Jesus wasn't blind. He
saw far more clearly into people's hearts than others did: he was
aware of their moral failings, their apparent spiritual indifference,
but such things did not change his attitude towards them, except to
make him care all the more. When he was challenged by the
guardians of morality concerning the company he kept, he replied
to them:

*'It is not the healthy that need a doctor, but the sick; I have
not come to call the virtuous but sinners to repentance.'*

~ Luke 5:31-32 ~

God knows each one of us far better than anyone else does, far
better than we know ourselves. He knows the things we so carefully
hide from other people; he knows the fears we find it hard to face;
he knows the times we have failed to live up to even our own best
standards; he knows how often we have been tempted to say, 'I
can't cope'; he knows the worst about us, but still he says, 'I want
you, just as you are'. That does not mean that he wants us to remain
as we are. He is out to get us, to refashion our lives into some-

thing finer than anything we yet know; but he wants us now, just as we are.

I want you, said God to Jeremiah, I want you just as you are, and I want you for my service. I have got a job for you to do; you are going 'to go to whatever people I send you, and say whatever I tell you to say'. So Jesus spoke to some fishermen and said, 'Come ... I've got a job for you to do' .... *'Come, follow me, and I will make you fishers of men'* (Mark 1:17).

A job to go to ... it's what many people in our society today are desperately wanting, and wanting in vain. One of the disheartening things about reading through the 'Situations Vacant' columns in our daily newspapers, is that if you are looking for a job you can read through column after column without coming across any job suitable for you – not my line, the wrong age, either under twenty-five or over forty, I haven't got the qualifications, they are looking for experience I don't have. One of the most important and heartening things about Christian service is that there is no one who can say it is not my line or I don't have the qualifications. There is only one qualification – the willingness to use the gifts which God has given us.

There is a story told about Principal David Cairns of Christ's College, Aberdeen, when he was visiting mission stations in Manchuria during his Moderatorial year. He was sitting on the veranda of a house one afternoon, having tea with some friends. The tea having been poured out, a Chinese boy came round with sugar.

'Two spoonfuls, please,' said David Cairns, and into his cup went two spoonfuls.

At that moment someone asked him a question and he began to talk. A moment or two later he picked up his cup, sipped the tea and said, 'Sugar please, two spoonfuls'.

Into his cup went another two spoonfuls. When the same thing happened again, this was more than the Chinese boy could stand:

'Don't give him any more,' he said. 'He has not stirred what he has got.' And that, I suspect, is the trouble with many of us.

A phrase I would like to see banished from our thoughts is the one behind which we hide so often – 'if only'. If only I had that other person's ability to speak; if only I found it as easy to make friends with other people as that other person does; if only I were as skillful with my hands; if only ... we have all thought it. If only .... But you are not that other person, and it is you, not someone else God wants to use. He wants to use what you have got, not what you haven't got. Aren't there things which you can do, which perhaps no one else can do or will do?

I don't normally keep letters. I have a large waste paper basket which is frequently filled and emptied. But I have kept three – all of them written by the same man, Revd Dr Arthur Gray, whose work in Bridgeton, Glasgow, and in other parishes is cherished by many people. They were letters written on different occasions, separated by many years. They were short, simple letters, typed on the same old typewriter, letters which had the remarkable ability to say the right thing at the right time. When Arthur Gray died, I discovered that there were countless other people who, like me, had received such letters, letters which had enriched the joy, the moments of success of many people; letters which had helped people to see the way ahead in difficult times; letters which had shared and lightened many a burden of grief and frustration. All because a man had taken time to sit down and type letters, which in many cases were to mean more to those who received them than ever he could have imagined. That was part of his ministry, part of the service God wanted and which he gladly gave.

Isn't there someone whom you can help, whose loneliness you can share: someone whose needs are known to you in a way known to no one else? A phone call you can make, a letter you can write, a visit you can pay; someone for whom you can pray? We sometimes think of the service of God as something which is done by the minister – you know, the person who wears, or used to wear, a dog-collar – or by a popular evangelist addressing a mass meeting at Murrayfield or the Kelvin Hall or Pittodrie, or by some prominent Christian who captures the headlines. For every such minister, evangelist or personality, however, there are hundreds of folk in every congregation called to do something which is ultimately far more vital for the kingdom of God; people with eyes to see what needs to be done in the name of Christ in the community around them; people prepared to use the opportunities and the gifts God has given them; people called to God's service every day.

There was a well-known American writer who, for much of the latter part of his life, fought a battle against a painful and debilitating illness. One day, when things were at their worst and he was deeply depressed, he sat down at his desk, took out a piece of paper and decided to write down on it the things upon which he could depend, the things which would never change, no matter how he was feeling. He sat for a long time and at the end was left with three brief sentences. Never mind what they were. I want to suggest that we would not go far wrong in our Christian experience if, following in the footsteps of Jeremiah, we summed up the unchanging, dependable truths of our faith in the following three simple statements:

God wants me,
> *God wants me just as I am,*
>> *God wants me for his service.*

The Closed Mind

~ Old Testament reading: Jeremiah 7 ~
~ New Testament reading: John 8:31-43 ~

THE two passages from the Bible which we read have one thing in common: they turn the spotlight on a curiously persistent inhabitant of the ancient and the modern world – people who happily live with the blinkered vision of a closed mind. The closed mind has had a long run for its money because it usually has a measure of truth in its make-up.

Take these people in Jerusalem who faced the threat of imminent invasion by gathering at the temple and saying: *'This place is the temple of the LORD, the temple of the LORD, the temple of the LORD .... We are safe!'* They had on their side a powerful religious heritage which past events had seemed to vindicate. Jerusalem in the past had survived against the odds, while equally important cities had bitten the dust. What further proof was needed of the faith of the Psalmist who declared, *'God is in that city, and it will never be destroyed'* (Psalm 46:5). The present crisis facing the community might be new, but God remained, present in their midst to protect them. So they could fling defiance in the face of their enemies.

Turn to the leaders of the Jewish community face to face with Jesus. They were right to claim they were privileged. They were heirs to a long and rich tradition of faith which marked them off from other people. They were the descendants of Abraham, the law of Moses directed their life, the teaching of the prophets and the psalmists was in their blood. In both cases here were people being true to long established religious beliefs, honouring their past, rejoicing in it. What then had gone wrong? Simply this – the past had become the prison of the present. They were set in their thinking, fighting all over again the battles of the past, instead of being open to the challenge of the present. Their minds were closed.

There are, of course, certain advantages in the closed mind, not least because it usually remains blissfully unaware that it is closed! It believes it has all the answers. It still has the indispensable pearls of wisdom for which the world is searching. Faced with people who, astonishingly, are neither grateful for its insights nor appreciative of its certainties, it takes refuge, not least in religious circles, in a host of colourful and vitriolic words which trip off the tongue with passionate assurance.

Many of us have been on the receiving end of such attacks. In the course of a radio phone-in during my moderatorial year, I was asked a question – a very reasonably put question by a girl whose home was in Stornoway – about the ferry Cal Mac which proposed to sail from Stornoway on Sunday. Since what was at stake was a way of life in the Western Isles, I emphasised that it was up to the local community to decide. I added, however, that I did not think that the rigid observance of the Sabbath, as practised in the Western Isles, was of the essence of the Christian Gospel. The response was swift and damning. The Presbytery of Lewis passed a vote of censure on a moderator who had dared to question their traditional, and what they believed to be the biblically-based, way of observing the Sabbath. In fact I had not attacked that view; I had only questioned whether it was a necessary part of the Gospel. If it is, then most Christians today throughout the world are being untrue to the Gospel. But on this issue no rational discussion was possible. Questioning was met with blanket, self-assured condemnation. I have hesitated to go on holiday to the Western Isles ever since!

There may be certain advantages in sheltering behind the certainties of the closed mind, but there are also certain disadvantages. Let me suggest one or two:

1 The closed mind is usually rooted in a failure to listen to what other people are saying. We can all be guilty of this. I once had the embarrassing experience of summoning to my office at the university a student whose work was very unsatisfactory. Attendance at classes was very irregular; several essays were long overdue. I knew something about him. I thought I knew what his problem was and set out at length to explain how he could solve it. He was very patient. Only after I had stopped delivering my words of wisdom did I discover that his problem was totally different from what I had imagined it to be. I could have saved myself not only embarrassment but time, if I had been prepared first to listen to what he had to say. One of the common charges that Jeremiah makes, in God's name, against the people of his day is '*they did not listen*' (*eg* Jeremiah 7:24). Often in religious circles the closed mind doesn't want to listen, indeed claims that it does not need to listen, since it already has all the answers.

'*This is the LORD's temple .... We are safe!*' – and any prophet who dares to challenge this assumption is ridiculed or ignored. '*We are the descendants of Abraham*' – and any man who asks awkward questions as to what this means is a threat to the status quo, and to be dismissed as a heretic or a traitor to his people's religion. Once you have found a suitably derogatory label to tie round someone's neck, you no longer need to listen to what he, or she, is saying. Religious institutions across the centuries have thus killed their prophets as well as their heretics … or have confused the two. It is easier to silence the challenging voice than to listen to what it has to say. How much more comfortable life would be, if only people who say or do outrageous things would go away or be silenced. We could then ignore the basic humanity we share with them.

A young Israeli soldier walks along a street just outside the walls of the old city of Jerusalem. Casually, but deliberately, he kicks over a basket of fruit which a Palestinian woman has laid out on the pavement to sell. He doesn't look at her; he doesn't need to. She is already labelled – a Palestinian Arab, a potential threat to the security of the state. He doesn't see the plea or the anger in her eyes. His mind is closed. There has been, and is, an ever-deepening tragedy in modern Israel because people are thus conveniently labelled, with most Jews until recently no longer listening to the Palestinians, and most Palestinians having ceased to listen to the Jews. The ideological battle lines are drawn. Stones and bullets speak louder than words. Words may be heard, but there is no real listening. Anything said from the other side is treated with suspicion, dismissed as 'inflexible' or 'nothing new'.

It is, of course, always easy to look at such a situation from the outside and see the bitter consequences of this failure to listen; it is far less easy to admit that we too are often involved in the same non listening game. We have done it as Christians for centuries. We have attached labels to fellow Christians, whether the label be Roman Catholic, Anglican, Baptist, Free Presbyterian or Church of Scotland, and assumed we need not seriously listen to what others are saying because they will only be reflecting their own prejudices. One of the things which the ecumenical movement has challenged us to do is to explore beyond our own prejudices, and to discover that there is much that we can share in life and in witness when together we seek to listen to God. Likewise, through inter-faith dialogue, we are beginning to listen to what people of other faiths in our midst have to say to us. It is not surprising that for the churches, and for many people in them, this has been a slow and painful experience. It means accepting that the truth, the whole truth of the Christian faith, is not the possession of any one of us, of any one church, not indeed the sole possession of any one religion.

Not that this is a problem peculiar to the church. It is one which politicians of all parties need to face. Why is it that many people's first reaction to a Party Political broadcast on TV is to switch channels or to switch off? Given the party label, they know what's coming. They believe they could write the script themselves. They no longer expect to hear a constructive political dialogue. What they get is a destructive, often self-righteous confrontation, characterised by a refusal to listen to what others are saying, unless it be to score cheap, if sometimes clever debating points. To listen, of course, is dangerous. We might hear something we would prefer not to hear, something that might make us take a long hard look at ourselves.

2 This refusal to listen goes hand in hand with the fact that the closed mind is unwilling to face the risk of being wrong or the horror of admitting that it has been, or is, wrong. It is easier in life to believe in 'them' and 'us' and to assume that 'they' are willfully wrong – when of course they differ from us – and that 'we' are usually reasonably right.

Glasgow has many claims to fame in addition to having been the European City of Culture. It has Barlinnie Prison. Within it there was the Special Unit which sought to rehabilitate offenders regarded as incorrigible under normal prison conditions. When it was instituted, it provoked some colourful descriptions in the popular press – 'Porridge with Cream', 'The Gilded Cage' – as if being in this unit was some kind of soft option. Listen, however, to one prisoner describing his experience of being in that unit:

> *It is a very difficult experience; you have got to be responsible for your own actions – and it is very painful. There is a sense of security in sub-culture values in prison, because people know how far to go with you. But here you have to strip yourself naked and you are vulnerable to everything, so vulnerable that it is unbelievable .... Here you have to admit your own guilt, and that is not easy when you are used to pleading not guilty to everything for so long. And when it is your own kind who are the judges that makes it even worse. Before, it was a 'them' and 'us' situation, but here that does not exist.*

These are the words of a man who had to come to terms with newly-given freedom and responsibility. They are very perceptive words. The closed mind always wants to take refuge in a plea of 'not guilty'. It needs the security of a sub-culture whether it is that of fellow prisoners or a group of like-minded believers or a political party or a nation. It is there in our biblical passages. '*This is the temple of the LORD .... We are safe*' – and here we shall defiantly huddle together, 'not guilty' in the face of the threat from pagan outsiders. '*We are the descendants of Abraham*' – and as for the rest, they are not.

Here let us remember a distinctively Christian insight which we neglect at our peril, the insight traditionally called the doctrine of original sin. Whatever we may think about the way in which this doctrine of original sin has been spelled out across the centuries, it does point us, without any shadow of doubt, to one lasting truth. The verdict of 'not guilty' is not one that any of us have any right to pass on ourselves. Our motives are too mixed, our insights too limited and at the mercy of prejudice, our practice so often out of line with our protestation, that we always stand in the need of confession. But confession is anathema to the closed mind, because confession demands that we face disturbing truths not only about other people but about ourselves. It reminds us that we dare not believe that we can solve our personal problems, or the problems of the society in which we live, by loading guilt solely upon other people, by identifying others as the source of all evil, questioning their every motive, while insisting that our hands are unsullied and our motives pure.

This does not mean that we should ever apologise for having deeply-held convictions, arguing openly for them and taking our stand by them. But convictions are different from blinkered dogmatism. Convictions are there to be tested and to be constantly re-examined in the light of experience and changing circumstances. Convictions are the launching pad for a journey capable of taking on board new insights. It has been claimed that Christian doctrines are excellent sign-posts, but bad hitching-posts. Sign-posts have been put there by people who have travelled this way before us. They point to the way we must travel if we seek to follow in their footsteps. They ask us to believe that they are pointing in the right direction. Follow them and we sometimes find ourselves travelling along roads we have never travelled before, facing new challenges and widening our horizons. Hitching-posts, however, tether us to where we are, useful enough as long as we wish to stay there, but never an invitation to set out in faith on a journey.

'*This place is the temple of the* Lord, *the temple of the* Lord, *the temple of the* Lord' – chant it three times and its emotional appeal is intensified: '*We are safe!*'

But these words remain the words of people tethered to the past. Within twenty years of that cry, the past was buried; the temple upon which they had placed their hopes was a charred ruin, and far from being safe they were in distant exile. Life has a nasty habit of doing that to the closed mind. The challenge posed by Jesus to those who believed they were the descendants of Abraham, was the challenge to become like Abraham – not to remain imprisoned in the past, but, as a follower of Jesus put it, to be like Abraham who '*obeyed the call to leave his home for a land which he was to receive as a possession; he went away without knowing where he was going …. For he was looking forward to a city with firm foundations, whose architect and builder is God*' (Hebrews 11:8,10). But to 'look forward' is to be open to the future, to journey and, who knows, perhaps to travel with some strange companions along the way.

It is the risk which is built into the serious study of any discipline, not least theology. I have long believed that the only person for whom a course in theology is a total failure, is the person who comes out at the end thinking in exactly the same way as he or she did at the beginning. That is the closed mind, closed to the varied riches of Christian tradition, closed to the many splendoured pattern and experience of Christian life and thought across the centuries. As Lesslie Newbigin has put it, faith can only be 'sustained in its integrity by the intellectual vigour and the practical courage with which its members seek to be faithful to it – not by repeating past formulas, but by courageously restating the tradition in the light of new experience'.

That is the risk to which we commit ourselves by becoming members of the Christian community; the risk of having our minds prised open, of having our horizons widened, and our lives enriched by others. It is the risk … but it is also the reward which must ever elude the closed mind.

The Goodness of God

How good God is to the upright,
How good to those who are pure in heart.

THESE, the opening words of Psalm 73, are words of apparently untroubled certainty and confidence. 'How good God is ....' But do you find it easy to talk about the goodness of God in the world in which we live today? Do these words come naturally to your lips even when, with the Psalmist, you are invited to assume that there is some kind of divine preferential system which ensures that such goodness is directed mainly towards God's people, towards 'the upright' and 'the pure in heart'?

The problem is sharply focussed for us in the events which compete for the headlines in our daily newspapers: if you were a mother in Somalia, cradling in your arms, clasping to a milkless breast a child dying of starvation and its associated diseases; if you were in Sarajevo, or in many a village in Bosnia, your home shelled, relatives shot or deported, women raped: if you were gazing at the twisted remains of a bomb-wrecked car in which a member of your family had died or been seriously maimed; or had witnessed a near neighbour gunned down in cold blood for no better reason than that he or she happened to be a Roman Catholic or a Protestant – would you find it easy to join in the anthem, 'How good God is ....'?

When we think of the personal tragedies which come to good

and bad alike, to the upright and the shifty, to the pure in heart and to the unscrupulous, to rich and to poor, to those who profess faith in God and to those who don't, do you find yourself saying with an easy conscience, 'How good God is to the upright .... How good to those who are pure in heart ....'? I don't.

What then are we to say about the author of this Psalm? Is he living in a world of self-deception, conveniently closing his eyes to much that is going on in the world around him? Is he wallowing in the sloppy sentimentality of an ill thought-out faith which has never seriously tried to come to terms with the harsh realities of life? Not at all: here is a man who has looked at life and found it twisted, grossly unfair and almost meaningless. The world he knew was a world in which ruthless arrogance and abuse of power seemed to pay handsome dividends, where the wicked made it to the top of the ladder and people with little or no conscience basked in success and popularity:

> *No pain, no suffering is theirs; they are sleek and sound in limb; they are not plunged in trouble as other men are, nor do they suffer the torments of mortal men.*   ~ Psalm 73:4-5 ~

People around him who openly ignored or flung defiance in the face of God, prospered and went on prospering. There were times when the words 'How good God is .... ' had almost stuck in this Psalmist's throat. He himself had been taken by suffering to the edge of a dark abyss. He had gazed into it and had been left asking whether it made any sense to continue to believe in the goodness of God. Far from bringing him confidence and inner peace, his belief in God at times added to the agony of life for him. I suspect that if we have never stood near the edge of that abyss, never been haunted by that same question and torn apart by something of that same agony, we are far from knowing what true faith means. Is there

71

any point in trying to hold on to a belief in the goodness of God when there is so much in the world which seems to call such a belief into question? The Psalmist was seriously tempted to answer, 'No, there is no point' – but he was checked by one stubborn fact which he could not deny. There *were* people he knew, people whom he respected, who did just that, who went on believing in the goodness of God in spite of so much that seemed to be pointing in another direction. Presumably they were not all spiritual or intellectual nincompoops!

That's one good reason for belonging to the church, to be able to draw on the experience and the faith of other people. So the Psalmist becomes conscious that there were two roads he could not travel. There was no way of holding onto belief in God and his goodness by looking at the world through rose-tinted spectacles – injustice and suffering were too much part of his experience for that: and there was no way in which he could easily renounce a faith which meant so much to other people, presumably just as sensitive as he was to the evil in the world. But to rule out these easy options hardly solved his problem. He stops … in doubt, confused and troubled. '*I set my mind,*' he says, '*to understand this, but I found it too hard for me ….*' (Psalm 73:16)

The Psalmist has had many companions across the centuries. He has many fellow travellers today – sensitive and honest people who have sat down to think this one out and found it too hard. As a merely intellectual dilemma it is insoluble. But for the Psalmist the way through did not come solely by sitting and thinking. It seldom does. Something happened to him. He went one day to the temple to worship, and there found himself grasped by a transforming experience of the reality of God's presence in his life. In the midst of his unanswered questions, while still struggling to come to terms with the cruel meaninglessness of much that he saw and experienced, he found himself saying … almost to his own surprise:

Yet I am always with you; you hold my right hand. You guide me by your counsel and afterwards you will receive me with glory. Whom have I in heaven but you? And having you, I desire nothing else on earth. Though heart and body fail, yet God is the rock of my heart, my portion for ever.

~ Psalm 73:23-26 ~

He was discovering that the bedrock of faith was not his puzzled, uncertain grasp of God, but God's sure grasp of him. He is not denying or turning a blind eye to the evil in the world, but he is defiantly affirming in the face of it, in the very midst of it, another certainty – the presence of God. This for him is the goodness of God, in the light of which everything else must be seen.

But, you may say, is this not just a cop-out, a pious form of escapism? Of course he claims to find God's presence in the temple; that is surely what worship is all about. There is nothing easier than to sit in the quiet beauty and serenity of a church, and there to affirm in word, in prayer and in song, the presence of God. This is where we expect to meet God, separated from the raw, ragged and uncomfortable questions of the world which for a few comforting moments we leave outside. If that is your experience, it is not mine, at least not often. I don't think the members of a Kirk Session, with which I was once associated, were untypical when in response to the question 'What do you find most unsatisfying in the life of the church?', they answered 'worship'.

I have shared in many acts of worship and been conscious of a whole host of things other than the presence of God – irritation with the preacher; a mind wandering over a hundred and one totally irrelevant thoughts; boredom … yes – but the presence of God? To be honest, not always, perhaps not often.

I would not wish for one moment to deny that as we gather for worship a sense of the presence of God may come to us, but I want to direct your attention to a challenging paradox. It is this. It has often been in the midst of what has seemed soul-destroying tragedy, and in the presence of the very things which raise questions about the goodness of God, that the presence of God has been most surely experienced and discovered. Who is more certain of the presence of God; who more radiates the presence of God? You and I as we sit together in this church; or Mother Teresa walking amidst and responding to the suffering and destitution in the streets of Calcutta? Not that Mother Teresa would for one moment deny the need for, or the value of, worship or the practice of the presence of God through worship. It is in her whole life, however, that she is affirming the presence of God, and if we cannot affirm it in the whole of life, it will escape us here.

A Jewish survivor of the Auschwitz death camp describes the day when the SS publicly executed three of his fellow Jews, two of them adults, one a young boy:

> *To hang a young body in front of thousands of spectators was no light matter. The head of the camp read out the death verdict. All eyes were on the child. He was lividly pale, almost calm, biting his lips .... The three victims mounted together onto the chairs. The three necks were placed at the same moment within the nooses. 'Long live liberty,' cried the two adults. But the child was silent. 'Where is God? where is he?' someone behind me asked. At a sign from the head of the camp, the three chairs tipped over .... I heard a voice within me answer: 'Where is God? Here he is – he is hanging on the gallows'.*

Dare we say that? Dare we say anything else? It is not surprising that the same man who recounts that incident speaks of prayer in the following way:

74

I no longer ask of you either happiness or paradise, all I ask of you is to listen and let me be aware of your listening. I no longer ask you to resolve my questions, only to receive them and make them part of you.

~ E. Weisel, *One Generation After*, p 241 ~

Many years ago an open debate was held in the University of Aberdeen. It was on the perennial problem of evil, with two lecturers from the Department of Philosophy making the initial contributions. The first speaker ended his contribution with a quiet but deeply moving account of a family he knew, a family with one child, a girl four years old, a girl dying slowly but inexorably of what was then an incurable leukaemia. He spoke of the tensions within the family, of a mother's heartbreak and of a father's bitterness at what must have seemed a wasted, unfulfilled life. Then he added, 'How can you believe in *any* god, far less the god of love in whom Christians claim to believe'.

The second speaker responded: 'I see such things just as clearly as you do. I feel them just as deeply. I am troubled and perplexed, but there is also Jesus ....'

But there is also Jesus – a comment made by a man who was not then, and as far as I know, is not now a member of the church. It may seem a disarmingly simple, if not indeed a naive statement. But it isn't. It takes us as far as the gallows, to a man dying in the midst of the blind hatred and irrational fears of otherwise well-intentioned people. It speaks of a man whose life more than any other communicated the sense of the presence and the goodness of God, a man who was truly 'pure in heart', yet who died with the words, 'My God, my God, why have you forsaken me?' on his lips. It challenges us to believe that it is precisely there in the darkness, in that man Jesus on the gallows, that the goodness and the presence of God is to be most clearly seen.

That is why, when the first Christians thought of the cross, they did not talk about the heroism of Jesus or the triumph of the human spirit over evil; rather they said:

Consider how great is the love which the Father has bestowed on us …. This is what love really is: not that we have loved God, but that he loved us and sent his Son ….

~ 1 John 3:1; 4:10 ~

That is why Paul, gripped by the same truth, could defiantly and triumphantly declare:

I am convinced that there is nothing in death or life, in the realm of spirits or superhuman powers, in the world as it is or the world as it shall be, in the forces of the universe, in heights or depths – nothing in all creation that can separate us from the love of God in Christ Jesus our Lord.

~ Romans 8:38-39 ~

Because the cross assures us that the goodness of God can be part of our experience now, even in the midst of much that would otherwise be unbearably dark and threatening, it gives us confidence to look forward in lively hope to a day when this flawed world will find all its pain and suffering wholly transformed by that same goodness. That is what we celebrate when we gather for worship. That is what gripped the Psalmist when long ago he went into God's sanctuary.

❖

The Voice of Protest

IT has been claimed, not without reason, that the book of Job is one of the greatest books not only in the Bible but in all literature. Read it, preferably in a modern translation such as the Revised English Bible, and you can't fail to be impressed by its mastery of words and its rich imagery.

Here is Job describing the plight which has befallen him:

Yet as a falling mountainside is swept away,
and a rock is dislodged from its place,
as water wears away stone,
and a cloudburst scours the soil from the land,
so you have wiped out the hope of frail man ....

~ Job 14:18-19 ~

Or read chapter 28 with its magnificent picture of the mining skill and ingenuity of man who

... sets his hand to the granite rock
and lays bare the roots of the mountains;
he cuts galleries in the rocks,
and gems of every kind meet his eye;
he dams up the sources of the streams
and brings the hidden riches of the earth to light.

leading into the question ....

> *But where can wisdom be found,*
> *and where is the source of understanding?*   ~ Job 28:9-12 ~

But the greatness of the book does not lie simply in its literary quality. It is a book which is wrestling with a problem which is as old as the hills and which is with us still, especially if we claim to believe in God. If this is God's world, why is there so much in it which is cruel, unjust and apparently meaningless? If you come to the book expecting to find an easy answer to that question, you are going to be disappointed. Try to read the book and you may find yourself ending up with more questions than you had at the beginning. Indeed you may find yourself getting lost, somewhere along the way.

The book, however, begins with a simple story. There was a man called Job who had everything you could possibly want if you were looking for the good life in his day – a large family and ample possessions to support both himself and them in style. Family parties were frequent, well worth attending. Not only so, but here was an upright man, a man of moral integrity who took his religion seriously, a man who was a living example of all that the Old Testament means by *shalom,* the full rich life, *'the greatest man in all the East'* (Job 1:3). Here then was a man of whom anyone, including God, could be justly proud. And that is what we find God doing, holding up Job as a shining example of the good and godly life.

But not everyone is convinced. Enter a prosecuting counsel (Satan) who says to God, 'Of course Job is a good and godly man of whom you can be proud. Why shouldn't he be? He has got everything going for him; it obviously pays him to be good. But what would happen if life were to turn sour?'

'All right,' says God, 'let's put him to the test.'

One by one the blows fall. Property, possessions and family are all taken from him. Job responds with quiet acceptance:

'Naked I came from the womb,
naked I shall return whence I came.
The LORD gives and the LORD takes away;
blessed be the name of the LORD.'

~ Job 1:21 ~

God has every right to be pleased. The first test has been passed with flying colours.

But the case for the prosecution is not yet complete. Suppose, says the prosecutor, we turn the screw a bit tighter; suppose we hit him personally and not merely through his possessions and his family. So we find Job in the grip of a loathsome disease, with sores breaking out all over his body. When his wife suggests that the only thing to do is to end it all by committing suicide, Job responds, *'You talk as any impious woman might talk. If we accept good from God, shall we not accept evil?'* (Job 2:10). Second test passed with flying colours? ... well, perhaps.

As Job sits silently trying to come to terms with his suffering, he is joined by three friends. Since these friends are to play an important part in the rest of the book, let's think first about them.

They *are* his friends. They need not have come; but they came as true friends so often do when we are in trouble, when we are trying to cope with grief and tragedy; and we are grateful for such friends. At first they don't say anything; they don't need to say anything. It is enough that they are there, sharing in his suffering and grief, assuring him that he was not alone. They don't need to say anything until Job eventually cracks and all the bitterness and doubts, the unanswered questions and the anger come pouring out, as he curses the day on which he was born. He has reached the point where he feels compelled to say, and go on saying, 'I can't take any more; life's not worth living. Why has God picked on me? What have I done to deserve this pain and suffering?'

They are his friends, and they are friends who have all the answers. In various ways they will insist that this is God's world, ruled over by a just and caring God who has so ordered life that good people are rewarded, while evil people come to a sticky end. True, because we are human and inevitably fall short of God's standards, suffering may come to any of us as a part of God's discipline. Nevertheless people do get what they deserve: the innocent never perish, the upright are never destroyed. So the friends call upon Job to confess his sins, to repent and to trust that God will restore him to his former good life, assuming that he is the good and godly man he once was said to be. The friends are here expressing a deep and sincerely held faith, a faith which we find elsewhere in the Old Testament, a faith which people have held down the centuries and still do today. It is the faith we hear on the lips of disciples who, when faced with a man blind from birth, ask Jesus, *'Rabbi, why was this man born blind? Who sinned, this man or his parents?'* (John 9:1). It is the attitude which is there when people ask, when faced with tragedy, 'I wonder what he (or she) did to deserve that?'

As Job listened to his friends, all he could say was, 'I don't care how deeply you believe that, but it's not true. God can't be like that. There is nothing I have done which can possibly justify the extent of the suffering I am experiencing. Don't tell me I'm getting what I deserve. God, for reasons best known to himself, must have his knife into me. What you are saying just doesn't make sense of my experience'. His friends are shocked at Job's response. How dare he accuse God of being unjust? How dare he question what they had all been brought up to believe? And when Job refuses to budge, their shock turns to anger. Instead of offering Job sympathy, they go over to the attack; instead of trying to understand the depths of the crisis of faith he is facing, they regard him as a threat to their own faith. They have the answers and Job better accept them. It never enters their minds that they might be wrong. Job must be silenced or destroyed.

They make the mistake which people with a sincerely held faith often make. They assumed that their understanding of life was the only possible understanding. They have all the answers and any awkward facts or questions which don't fit their answers must be ignored or explained away. They came as friends to support Job; they end up shocked and angry, ready to damn Job and to rewrite his life to make it fit their script. Job had touched them on a raw spot. He was asking them to think again about what they believed, to be open to the possibility that their understanding of the ways of God might not be adequate to account for some of the grim facts of life. That's not something that any of us are very anxious to do. Yet sometimes it must be done. It is one of the great ironies of the book that at the end God turns to one of these friends who were so sure that they were speaking for God, and says to him, *'My anger is aroused against you and your two friends, because, unlike my servant Job, you have not spoken about me as you ought'* (Job 42:7).

So much for the friends, but what about Job? Perhaps one of the most important things about the book is that it has no easy answers to offer. Nowhere, from beginning to end, is there any neat explanation given as to why this world and human life is so often riddled with pain and suffering, or why we are frequently left facing things which just don't make sense. The friends have their answers; Job has little more than questions. The friends are sure about what they believe; Job is far from sure.

If that were all, it would be a very disturbing and upsetting book.

But two things still need to be said, two things which are there in the first words which God address to Job in the book:

Who is this who darkens counsel
with words devoid of knowledge?
Brace yourself and stand up like a man;
I shall put questions to you, and you must answer.

Where were you when I laid the earth's foundations?
Tell me, if you know and understand.
Who fixed its dimensions? Surely you know!
Who stretched a measuring line over it?
On what do its supporting pillars rest?
Who set its corner-stone in place,
while the morning stars sang in chorus
and the sons of God all shouted for joy?

~ Job 38:2-7 ~

The first thing we must learn to accept is that we don't, we *can't,* know all the answers to life's experiences, because we are not God. We are God's frail creatures, living for a short time in our own tiny corner of one of the smallest planets in a universe far greater than we can imagine. Even our ordinary everyday experience is surrounded with mystery:

There are colours that we shall never see because our vision lies between the violet and the red bands of the spectrum. Think what the world might be like if the human eye were sensitive to the ultra violet or the infra red or if we could see the electro-magnetic fields. There are sounds which we shall never hear for they are above or below the limited compass of the human ear .... We only pick up one in every thousand billion of the

82

vibrations which surround us and which pass through us without leaving a trace in our consciousness. There is a tremendous reality which lies beyond and which will always lie beyond the edge of our senses, so that our human consciousness is like a small spotlight moving over a dark landscape.

~ T. M. Taylor, *Where One Man Stands*, p 14 ~

We may ask our questions, we may protest that there is much that does not seem to make sense, we may protest to God or about God, as Job did, but we must learn to be humble before the mystery of life and be prepared to say, 'I don't know'. Martin Dalby, one of our most distinguished composers, once pointed to what music and religion had in common. 'Both,' he said, 'try to touch the senses with the magic of wonder .... Bad religion answers the unanswerable: great religion cherishes the mystery.' If you are ever tempted to think that you have God neatly labelled, and that you know exactly how he works out his purposes in the world, then read Job chapters 38-41. These chapters will make you think again. They won't provide you with easy answers, but they will put you in the place from which answers begin, as you bow in wonder before the awesome power and majesty of God, and learn to cherish the mystery. That is part of true faith. It is that which leads Job in the end to say:

... I have spoken of things
which I have not understood,
things too wonderful for me to know.

~ Job 42:3 ~

There are times when, if we are honest, we have to say, 'I don't know'.

There is, however, one thing that we can and do know. One of the things which most troubled Job was that, in the midst of his pain and suffering, he felt cut off from God. Again and again he found himself groping blindly for a God who seemed ever elusive, a God who must at least be just, but whom he could not reach.

> *If only I knew how to reach him,*
> *how to enter his court,*
> *I should state my case before him*
> *and set out my arguments in full;*
> *then I should learn what answer he would give*
> *and understand what he had to say to me.*
>
> … … …
>
> *If I go to the east, he is not there;*
> *if west, I cannot find him;*
> *when I turn north, I do not descry him;*
> *I face south, but he is not seen.*

~ Job 23:3-5, 8-9 ~

But in the end Job discovered that the God he could not reach, reached out for him. The God who had seemed silent and elusive, came and spoke; not to give neat answers to Job's questions, but to question Job. And in that questioning Job discovered he was no longer alone; God was there in the midst of his pain and suffering. He was no longer being attacked by shocked and angry friends – he was with God.

In the past, says Job:

> *I knew of you then only by report,*
> *but now I see you with my own eyes.*

~ Job 42:5 ~

It is that 'seeing', that sense of being with God, or rather of God being with us, that enables us to face the demands which life makes upon us, and helps us to live confidently and joyfully, even when we have many unanswered questions; especially since as Christians we know, as Job didn't and couldn't know, that *'the Word became flesh and dwelt among us'* (John 1:14), and dwells among us still in 'the Spirit of God who in all his glory rests upon us' (1 Peter 4:14).

Questions ...
and Questions

MALACHI is hardly one of the favourite, or best known, books in the Bible. Those of you who have sung in, or are otherwise familiar with Handel's 'Messiah', will know a few verses from it, including the famous aria 'But who may abide the day of his coming ....' Apart from that, I suspect that for most of us the book of Malachi is more or less a blank in our knowledge of the Bible. It has one thing in its favour, however: it is easy to find. You may stumble across it by accident when you are looking for Matthew's Gospel, the first book in the New Testament, since Malachi is the last book in the Old Testament. Even at that you better not blink, or you may miss it. It takes up only two pages in most of our Bibles, and even when you spin it out with an introduction and line drawings, as in the Good News Bible, it is still only three pages.

It is a short, crisp book written nearly five hundred years before the coming of Jesus. It comes from a man who concealed his identity under a pen name 'Malachi', Hebrew for 'my messenger', God's messenger, a description which could apply to many people, indeed to any prophet in the Old Testament. Read it through from beginning to end and you will find that it is a book full of questions and answers, or perhaps more accurately, questions ... and questions, questions of many different kinds. There are the questions which Malachi hears his people asking God. There are the questions which he believes God is asking his people. In the middle there is

Malachi himself, fielding some of the questions and tossing in a few awkward ones of his own.

Let us take a look first at some of the questions the people were asking God. They were questions being asked against the background of difficult and depressing times. Many of the hopes with which people had returned from exile to build a new and better Jewish community had been destroyed. They were in the grip of a recession and it was hard to see any signs of recovery just round the corner. They were questions being asked by a community which didn't quite know where it was going, a community in which people were in danger of losing their vision of God. Some of them are basic questions which people have always asked and still ask about God.

The book begins with a ringing declaration, '*I have shown you love, says the LORD*'. Fine words, but sometimes they take a bit of believing, don't they, when the going is tough; so it is not surprising that the people throw back in God's face the question, '*How have you shown love to us?*' (1:2). The world they knew and the challenging situation they were facing seemed cruel, puzzling and apparently meaningless; and it was not enough to be told that their plight was at least better than that of some other people. That is no real answer; so they go on to ask, '*Where is the God of justice?*' (2:17). It is hard not to ask such questions, isn't it, as the images flash across our TV screens – child abuse, violence and revenge killings in Northern Ireland, dehydrated dying children in many parts of Africa, Kurdish refugees, conflict in Israel .... In the midst of all this, if this is God's world, where is the God of justice and love? Sometimes the questions come home to us with a more sharply cutting edge, as in our own lives we are forced to face the tension which so often seems to exist between what we have been taught to believe about God, and the harsh reality we face.

Several years ago the BBC film 'Shadowlands' traced the happiness and the agony of a man who for many people had become one of the most convincing and entertaining defenders of the Christian faith – C. S. Lewis. Alone in his study, after the death of the woman he had so deeply and briefly loved, he found his own faith under threat and everything which he had so confidently and convincingly said to others being called into question. He wrote:

Where is God? Go to him when your need is desperate, when other help is in vain, and what do you find? A door slammed in your face, and a sound of bolting and double bolting on the inside. After that silence. You might as well turn away, the more emphatic the silence will become. There are no lights in the windows. It might be an empty house. Was it ever inhabited? It seemed so once ....

C. S. Lewis eventually won through to a deeper faith, but it was only after long, honest and agonising wrestling with the questions, 'Where is God?' and 'What does his love mean to me now?'

But how many others have faced, and still face, the same questions, and have never found an answer? 'How have you shown your love to us?' 'Where is the God of justice?' – searching questions, as real today as they were in Malachi's day.

We also, however, hear other questions on the lips of the people in Malachi's day – angry, defensive questions, hurled at God by people who wish to justify themselves:

'How have we despised your name?' (1:6)

'How have we wearied God?' (2:17)

'How have we defrauded you?' (3:8)

'What do we gain from the LORD of Hosts by observing his rules and behaving with humble submission?' (3:14)

These are the kind of questions which have been well described as 'words, words, words', pre-emptive strike words which do their best to ensure that we will not have to face awkward questions about ourselves. Carry the fight to the enemy just in case he gets in first. Sometimes one of the most comfortable and reassuring places in which to hide from God is in the midst of such questions.

There is nothing more enjoyable at times than having a good going religious argument. We lay God out, as it were, on the dissecting table. We view and examine the body. We check it out against standard text books with which we are familiar, whether it be the Bible, or the creeds of the church, or our own prejudices. We stand around and argue, coolly or dispassionately, hotly or intensely. Indeed, I never cease to be surprised how normally sane and mild-mannered people can get hot under the collar when they start arguing about religion, especially those who claim that religion is really a matter of indifference to them. We love playing a religious word game that may seem less trivial than some other pursuits, but is none the less fraught with danger.

The book of Malachi, however, and indeed the whole Bible, speaks to us of a God who has a disconcerting habit of getting up from the dissecting table on which we have put him, a God who comes not merely to listen to our questions as we stand around him, but a God who comes to stand before us to ask us questions. So, in Malachi, we come face to face with a God who is asking his people searching questions:

If I am a father, where is the honour due to me? If I am a master where is the fear due to me? (1:6)

When you buy a blind or sick or lame animal to sacrifice to me, do you think there is nothing wrong with that? Try giving an animal like that to the governor! Would he be pleased or grant you favours? (1:8)

And Malachi himself, God's messenger, breaks in to say to the people …

Have we not all one father? Did not one God create us? Why then are we faithless to one another ....? (2:10)

The one thing all these questions have in common is that they challenge the people to take a long hard look at themselves, their sense of values, their lifestyle and the way they treat others. This is no longer merely 'words, words, words' – this is the 'word of God' throwing down the gauntlet, questioning what life, your life, and my life, is all about. The questions God directs towards the people of Malachi's day are not vague, general questions about ultimate values. We may safely discuss such questions until doomsday and remain unchanged in our daily living. No, they are all personal, pointed questions, homing in on what the people in Malachi's day were doing or not doing.

There were the promises they had made to God to offer him the best when they came to worship. But they brought him as sacrifices the scraggiest animals they could lay their hands on. Times were hard after all; they were in a recession, they had to think of themselves and their families. How often have we made similar excuses for the poverty of our worship, our giving, our service to God?

Once we stood before a congregation and heard the question:

'Do you promise to make diligent use of the means of grace, to share dutifully in the worship and service of the church, and to give of your substance, as the LORD may prosper, for the advancement of his kingdom throughout the world?'

We heard and we answered, 'I do'.

Do we? If so, we are among the minority of members of the church today. Can any of us face that question with a clear conscience?

There were the promises people in Malachi's day had made to each other, promises, for example, of fidelity – and they were not paying much attention to such promises. They could hardly deny what they were doing, but they did it with a shrug of their shoulders. After all, it was none of God's business, was it? If that is what we want in life, an attitude which says 'it is nobody's business but my own what I do with my life', then you can't get it from the God who comes to us in and through the Bible.

There was a young man who came to Jesus one day who wanted something like that. He was quite happy to have a discussion about religion with Jesus, a serious and deep discussion: '*What must I do to win eternal life?*' (Luke 18:18ff). He could handle the discussion so long as it remained at the level of the general religious teaching which had been part of his upbringing. Yes, he knew the commandments, yes he lived by them – and in this he was totally sincere. It was when Jesus moved from such general religious teaching to face him with a personal choice he had to make, a choice which raised questions as to where his priorities lay at that moment, that the going became tough and he could no longer face it. Luke comments, 'when he heard this, his heart sank'.

It is dangerous to play about with religious questions. Questions about God have a nasty habit of spilling over into questions about ourselves. Indeed, perhaps questions about God are not real questions until they do just that.

Do we have questions about how God loves us? Then they are really questions about the way in which we are prepared to live, whether we are prepared to take the risk of loving in the way in which we have seen such love in Jesus.

Do we ask, 'Where is the God of justice?' Then we are really asking, 'What are we prepared to do – to work, to give, to pray – so that all people in God's world shall have a chance to experience justice and that fulness of life through which they can share many of the things we take for granted – freedom, food, shelter, medical care, education ....?'

There are many questions we need to ask and go on asking about the world in which we live, especially if we believe it to be God's world:

- ... questions about famine in Africa and elsewhere, and the extent to which the problem is insoluble unless corrupt governments and civil war are eliminated;
- ... questions about energy and population problems: questions about the assumption of politicians of all parties who seem to think that all we want to hear is the promise of more and more for ourselves, as if we had little or no responsibility for the developing countries, caught in a poverty trap, crippled by the terms of world trade and debt repayment;
- ... questions about the belief that market forces rule the world and our economy, and that people can be sacrificed on the altar of such forces.

There are questions to be asked and political solutions to be sought, *but* if in a world in which there is so much that is loveless and unjust we dare to believe in a God of love, whose justice and compassion reach out to embrace all his children, *all* his children, then we have got to look at ourselves, question our priorities, our lifestyle, and ask whether we are being the channels of such love, compassion and justice. That can happen, or not happen, in the simplest of ways.

Archbishop Tutu, born and brought up in the poverty and squalor of black townships in South Africa, describes one of the moments which changed his life. He was walking with his mother along a dusty road when a white man, dressed in a long white cassock, wearing a black hat, came towards them. As he passed by he lifted his hat to Desmond Tutu's mother. That a white man could do that to a black woman made a profound and lasting impression on him. Ever since, it has coloured his attitude to relationships between black and white. That man was Trevor Huddleston, Anglican priest, like Tutu, for many years the voice of the voiceless oppressed in South Africa.

More than perhaps anyone knew at the time, God's love and concern for justice were there in the simple lifting of a hat. If they are not there in our daily actions, we are back where the people in Malachi's day were, hiding behind their hang-ups about God, but really saying we don't mean the promises we have made. To have a mind full of questions about God, and to be deaf to questions about ourselves, is the ultimate betrayal of faith.

About the Author

ROBERT DAVIDSON MA, BD, DD, FRSE was born in Fife, Scotland and educated at the University of St Andrews. He lectured at Aberdeen, St Andrews and Edinburgh Universities before becoming Professor of Biblical Studies at the University of Glasgow. He was Moderator of the General Assembly of the Church of Scotland in 1990 and served as the Interim General Secretary of the Church of Scotland Department of Education. He is currently involved with Action of Churches Together in Scotland.

SAINT ANDREW PRESS

ON REFLECTION ...

Duncan Forrester (series editor)

Other titles available in this series